Who Would Have Thought...

by
Sheri Rose Shepherd
Mrs. United States 1994~95

with
Steven Gene Shepherd
and
Tom DiBiase

Ingram Distribution
TriStar Printing
A Shepherd Publication

Cover Photos by Deanna Graham
Publicity Photos by Richard Petrillo

Robin & Steven

Enjoy Life!

Life a Gift

7/95

Sherw Rose Shephnel

WHO WOULD HAVE THOUGHT

A Shepherd Publication

Printed June, 1995

ISBN:

0-9647475-0-2

PRINTED IN THE UNITED STATES OF AMERICA

"...and our new Mrs. United States is...
Sheri Rose Shepherd!"

Preface

The master of ceremonies held up the envelopes containing the winner's names and announced, "Our new Mrs. United States of America is...Mrs. Arizona! Sheri Rose Shepherd!"

In that instant, when I heard my name, I screamed, I cried, I lost all of the control and composure I'd had been trying to display during the competition. I just couldn't believe it had actually happened. I was the new Mrs. United States!

I know that some people see me and think, "She's just another 'beauty queen' desperately trying to exalt herself," or maybe, "So what, you won a national title!" Others question why in the world I'd ever enter a pageant! I've even heard women say, "How can a person who enters beauty pageants call herself a Christian?"

I wish for a moment they could walk in a pair of shoes from my past. They might then see this victory from a different point of view. They would see that this is not just a victory over physical beauty. Nor is it a triumph over fifty other women on a brightly lit stage. The crown, the banner, the title and the reign represent only a temporary flame that will soon, no doubt, be outshone by another.

To understand the significance of that night, and the intensity of that moment, you would have to adjust your gaze out of the spotlight, off of the stage, and onto a little girl weeping lonely, desperate tears under the stars on a front porch step.

I cried myself to sleep practically every night. Not just because of the violent, destructive home I lived in, but because I suffered from hopelessness. As a teenager, I was fifty pounds overweight, addicted to drugs and struggled with chronic depression. I soon fell victim to bulimia and, at age 24, I decided to end my life.

I tell my story to thousands of people, not because I'm a beauty queen who loves the attention—far from it. My story is personally humiliating because my life is full of mistakes, bad choices and damaged relationships. It isn't easy exposing my weaknesses to the world.

I share my story because I understand the emotions of the bulimic who can't control her compulsion, the drug abuser who can't stop the addiction, the overweight, insecure teenager suffering from depression and the person who carries the excess baggage of abuse from the past.

This book is **NOT** a 10-step program on how to win a pageant. Nor is it a sob story about my struggles with suicide, depression and failure, but instead, it's a journey. A journey of transformation and personal growth; of laughter and surprise.

Sheri Rose Shepherd
June, 1995

Chapter 1

Setting The Stage

I grew up in one of the craziest, most unusual and eccentric families you could ever imagine. My Jewish Grandfather escaped from Russia and ended up in America to start a family. My grandmother ended up in the hospital.

"It's a tumor," pronounced Doctor #1. Things couldn't be worse. But, thanks to medical breakthroughs like the Second Opinion, Doctor #2 grabbed the X-ray and announced, "this isn't a tumor! It's a baby!"

My father's surprise entrance to the world was incredibly fitting. He always makes a grand entrance—living up to his "Hurray for Hollywood" image. Everything had to be done bigger, better and different from anyone else. Let me give you a peek at the insanity I grew up in....

While most little girls might receive a cute little stuffed animal as a token of their father's affection, my father would have live animals such as elephants, horses, and camels delivered to the doorstep of our home. My dad got a kick out of the entire state of California watching his extravaganza broadcast on the six o'clock news.

Greeting cards weren't good enough for Dad either. He'd pay to have huge billboards on major California highways plastered with his words of adoration. Also, I remember on Fourth of July when he bought out the entire inventory from every fireworks stand he could find. He then generously distributed them to every neighborhood kid on our block. The only condition was that the kids had to set them all off at once!!

If you had been one of my neighbors back then, you'd have probably run out to get the most expensive homeowner's insurance policy you could possibly afford, because, you never knew just what my dad might be bringing to the neighborhood from week to week.

I think my dad's greatest thrill is being a hero. He had a childhood passion for the Lone Ranger, and seemed to spring to life with super-human strength whenever he was faced with an heroic rescue.

My Dad's "memory building" experiences weren't limited to his family, either. He once overheard the secretaries in his San Diego office complaining that they missed the snow in the winter. The next day, he surprised them by hiring an ice company to blow six tons of snow in the company parking lot! They threw snow balls and laughed like children as they shared with the TV news cameras about their zany boss, Phil Goodman. Once again, the Lone Ranger saves the day!

Dad would go to any extreme to "blow people's minds". Once, at his own office birthday party, he ran out in the middle of the street, ripped off his clothes down to his underwear and threw his birthday cake in his own face! It's a wonder my dad hasn't been hauled off to the looney bin!

As for my mom, she was a former beauty queen, and once had her own television show called *Rosie*. She was incredibly gorgeous. She could sing, she could dance, she could act—I thought she could do it all. But the one thing she did not know how to do was love or be loved. As a child, she was severely abused emotionally and physically. As a result, she found it impossible to express her love for me. When I'd say, "I love you, Mommy," she'd say, "No, you don't!" No matter how hard I tried, I could not win her affection. I felt like an outsider, constantly rejected. It was as though I were living with this beautiful stranger whom I could not get close to.

Both my parents are graduates of Hollywood High School, and their relationship started out a lot like a Hollywood script. When my dad first met my mom, he thought she was the most beautiful thing he'd ever laid eyes on. He didn't seem to care that she was already married and had two young boys. He didn't even consider the fact that she was 26 and he was only 19. He went so "nuts" over her that he didn't even mind their religious differences. All he knew was that he loved her more than life itself, and that he would do anything to win her hand in marriage.

Back then, my father was a disc jockey for KBLA in Los Angeles, and was famous for doing extremely successful live remote broadcasts for the station's advertisers. He even used to get Mom in on the act, dressing them both up in outrageous costumes to stand in front of the advertiser's place of business to entice people inside (don't all parents start their mating ritual like this?). Mom told me that Dad, clad in a gorilla outfit, ran out into the street to stop traffic and then would say to the stunned occupants, "If you don't come in and buy something, I'm going to bite your stomach off!" Talk about going the extra mile for your client!

Believe it or not, my mom loved my dad's outrageous sense of humor. She saw in him the spark of excitement she wanted in her life. So she packed up her two boys, left her husband, and ran off with my eccentric father.

In so many ways, they seemed perfectly suited for one

another. Only a few obstacles stood in their way. First of all, my dad had been supporting his parents. He was afraid to tell them that "on impulse" he'd run off and married an older woman with two children—a woman who wasn't exactly the nice Jewish girl they'd always dreamt he'd bring home. So, he decided to live part-time with his new wife and part-time with his parents. He told his parents that his job kept him on the road a lot.

If it weren't tough enough just trying to balance a double life, my dad had to work three jobs to support his new family as well as his parents. The unbearable stress of his new life overtook him and he developed a severe temper, eventually becoming a walking time-bomb that would explode at the least little thing.

Dad's temper paralyzed my mother with fear. Her dream man, who was supposed to fill her days with excitement and romance, had turned into a nightmare. But just when they were ready to end their marriage, my mother became pregnant. Yes, it was me!

My insane father in the middle of the street, after smashing his birthday cake in his own face!

Snowing in San Diego? Only my dad would blow six tons of snow in his office parking lot because his secretaries missed winter.

My very own billboard, instead of a birthday card from Dad, on Highway 17 in San Jose, California.

Dad played boogie woogie in piano bars at 15 and was a DJ in Los Angeles at 19. (No, the girl is not my mother.)

My dad in 1958, doing a live radio promo-
tion with some beauty pageant girls.

At the Station with Dad. He had me doing
radio commercials at age 2.

Chapter 2

What A Way To Start!

Because their lives had become such a mess, my mother was terrified of having a baby with my father. She realized, though, that she had nowhere else to go. My dad felt as though his youthful dreams and fun times would come to a screeching halt, but, he too, felt stuck. He now had three children in the house to support, along with a wife and two sick parents, and there were no more hours in the day to fit a fourth job.

As a little girl, I cannot remember even one peaceful night in our home. All I remember is hearing my parents fighting, screaming, and abusing each other. Just about every night, I'd crawl in bed and cry myself to sleep. I wanted so badly for the fighting to stop.

My father wanted it to stop too, but, his way of dealing with it was slightly out of control. He'd call all of us into the living room and scream at us as loudly as he could, "I demand instant happiness! I deserve to be happy! Be happy right NOW, and I mean it!" He made us afraid to express our true feelings.

Later on, I remember breaking one of mom's favorite lamps. She was so mad, she refused to speak to me for more than a week. My dad, annoyed with the childish, silent treatment, sprang to action with one of his more memorable solutions to our endless family disputes. He demanded that mom and I gather up every remaining lamp in the house and place them together in the back yard. He then went into a tirade about "lamps tearing our family apart", handed us both sledgehammers and insisted that we demolish every lamp we owned! I can't say I learned a lot from dad's interesting lesson in family communication, but mom and I had an absolute, hysterical, laughing fit swinging those stupid hammers around! Of course, we both had to then rush to the lamp store with dad, the hero, to buy bigger and better lamps.

Often after one of his huge explosions of temper, Dad would feel guilty, so he would take us all out shopping and tell us, "Buy whatever you want!" He didn't understand that a simple, sincere "I'm sorry" would have done far more to repair the damage than unlimited credit on a bank card could.

My only refuge as a little girl was in the arms of my father's father, who I affectionately referred to as my 'Da Da'. I loved spending time with him. Actually, both my grandparents gave me their undivided attention, but there was a special place in my heart for my grandpa. He was so kind and gentle. He'd give me 'tickles' on my back and play with me until the wee hours of the morning.

He just loved to spoil me—partly, I think, because he knew what my home life was like. He tried his hardest to make my time with him as special as possible. He started by turning his back yard into my own private playground. I told him I liked to play in the sand, so he had a huge sandbox built just for me. I said I liked birds, so he had a pigeon coop built with over forty birds in it for me to play with. If I told him about a toy I wanted, he'd run out and buy it for me.

When I think about my 'Da Da', I know I didn't love him because he spoiled me. When I was with him, I felt safe. In my eyes he was the most wonderful person on earth.

My loving grandparents, Archie and Sadie Goodman, holding me for the first time in 1961.

At age four, I was already pretending to be a beauty queen. I would dress up in heels and a swimsuit and try to walk straight.

I loved playing with dolls as a little girl. I'd hide out on the back porch step sometimes when my parents were fighting.

The love of my life was my grandfather, my "Da-da".

Chapter 3

A Strange Way to Say You Love Me

When I was four, my mom and dad came home with my new baby brother, Michael. They were so excited about their new son, yet, I felt somewhat rejected. It wasn't long before I noticed there was something more than just a new baby brother that felt different. I had grown used to hearing the echo of angry, hateful fighting, but for now, the house remained silent. No one wanting to wake the baby.

Peace and Quiet were welcome guests yet, even with a baby around, it didn't last for long. Many times I remember lying in bed, holding my baby brother tightly, while Mom and Dad fought with each other until all hours of the night.

I wanted to run away from all the violence, but I didn't know where to go. Often, when visiting my grandparents, I'd conveniently lose my shoes. I figured that, if I couldn't find them when my parents came to get me, then maybe I wouldn't have to leave so soon. I loved my grandparents and cherished every moment we were together.

Then one day, my father came home with some big news. "I've been offered a job as sales manager at a radio station! It'll pay twice as much as all three of my other jobs put together, and with regular hours," he exclaimed. "Before you get too excited," he continued, "...we're moving to Modesto, California." At this news, I ran to my room and slammed the door. Dad followed to see what was the matter.

"I want to stay here with Grandpa and Grandma," I cried. "I don't want to go with you." He tried to comfort me, but it was no use. I was convinced I'd never be happy again. The only joy I'd ever known as a child was my time with my grandparents, and I resented my parents for moving away from them.

After the move, my dad was able to spend more time at home, and this only served to make the fighting even worse. I began turning to food for comfort. It seemed all I ever did was eat and cry, eat and cry. Sometimes, I'd come home from school and eat an entire box of *Cap'n Crunch* cereal, ten pieces of bread, and some raw cookie dough. I'd sit glued to the TV watching the Brady Bunch, wishing I could be in *their* family instead of mine.

My mother became increasingly depressed and lonely, and she started dating other men to try and meet her deep need for love and affection. It was incredibly difficult for me to see my mom affectionately touching another man, especially because I so desperately wanted my parents to love each other that way.

Sometimes I felt like telling my dad what was going on, but I just couldn't. He'd be crushed, and we seldom talked as it was, since I was so afraid of his violent temper.

When I was eight, we moved again, this time to Sacramento, where Dad had been offered an even better job as the sales manager of a TV station. Mom began working as a nurse in a local hospital. It wasn't long, however, before she started seeing one of the doctors she had met there.

In an attempt to keep me occupied, Mom forced me to take baton lessons, ballet lessons, piano lessons, gymnastics, and swimming. I was so overweight and depressed that I was usually pretty bad at these things. The other kids made fun of me, and even some of the teachers put me down.

When Mom saw these activities were only making me frustrated, she gave up and let me stay home after school each day with my stepbrother, David. At age 15, David was not ready to take on such a responsibility. He'd grown up under the tyranny of my father. He hated life, and he had turned to marijuana to try and numb his pain.

I really loved David and I always thought he was "cool". When I saw him smoking pot with his friends, I wanted to join in, and he let me. He didn't care. I actually started abusing drugs at the tender age of nine! As long as I was "high", I didn't have to feel anything or deal with the pain. The usual important things like, life, relationships and responsibility were magically drained of their power and became "no big deal". Smoking pot also increased my appetite tenfold, and I started eating more than ever. So in addition to frying a few billion brain cells, I was getting bigger and bigger with every passing day.

Then came another crisis that pushed me completely over the edge. My beloved grandfather died of a heart attack. This grieved me so deeply, I wanted to die myself. Although they tried, no one was able to comfort me. I loved my grandpa more than anyone in the world. How could he die? How could he leave me to face the world alone?

A few months after Grandpa's death, my mother and I were sitting at the kitchen table when she began to tell me about one of her patients at the hospital. "He's such a wonderful old man, just like your grandpa was. I've told him all about you, and he wants to meet you." Since the hospital was just across the street from my school, I agreed to stop in and see him the next afternoon.

I entered his room expecting to see someone like my grandfather, but what I saw was a man who was moments from death, connected to life support machines with tubes coming from everywhere. His appearance horrified me. I yelled bitterly at my mother, "Why did you bring me here?"

"He wanted to see you, Sheri," she replied.

"I hate you! I hate you!" I screamed as I ran home as fast as I could, crying my eyes out.

For weeks afterward, I had terrible nightmares about death. I kept picturing my grandpa the way I saw that man in the hospital. It got to the point where I was afraid of falling asleep. My mother tried to tell me, "Death is a part of life. You need to learn to accept that." As a nine year-old, I just couldn't deal with the hopelessness of it. I was far too young to understand.

This is the only family photo we ever took together.

I remember really looking up to my big brother, David. Here we are with new brother, Michael.

At first, I wasn't too thrilled about sharing Mom with my new baby brother, Michael.

I still remember being mistaken for a boy while I was skiing. Here, I let my hair down to leave no room for doubt.

I cuddled with my neighbor's kitten at age 9. I was chubby, even then.

I was a very depressed sixth grader. This photo was taken shortly after my grandfather's death.

Chapter 4

Fame, Fortune & Beauty

Thanks to my mixed-up and often wacky family, I learned some outrageous lessons about things like money, success and vanity.

Take "looks", for example. Everybody can relate to a bad hair day, but my dad was extreme. His hair was rather fine with a bit of a wave, which he hated. He was positively obsessed with getting it just so. He often would—I'm not making this up—spend a full hour-and-a-half blow-drying it to "get all the 'dents' out," as he put it. We'd joke that he only had three pieces of hair anyway and spent a half-hour on each one. He had a special round brush he'd use to painstakingly manipulate his hair into the shape he sought. And woe to the poor soul who made the mistake of using or moving the sacred implement.

For Mom, a big hang-up was the "age" thing—getting older. To be fair, she probably handled being thirty-something about as well as most people. It's just that, at the time, it was incredibly embarrassing for me to have my mom pick me up at my school wearing a skimpy skating outfit and ice skates with the guards on. I think she really liked the attention. I'll never forget the time she grounded me because I told someone how old she was.

As for "fame", my father's connections—and his aggressive behavior—allowed us to meet some pretty big stars from time to time. I remember meeting the King of Rock and Roll, Elvis Presley backstage in Lake Tahoe after one of his shows. I also remember meeting Helen Reddy, the Osmond Brothers (Donny gave me one of his purple socks!), and the Jackson-Five. My dad once got me backstage to meet a young Michael Jackson and even arranged to have Michael tape a special interviewed recording just for me.

As for "money", I've already told you a little about the shopping sprees. Dad would take us to buy clothes and let us get anything and everything we wanted. We'd walk up to the cashier, each carrying mounds of stuff, and, as a joke, Dad would be carrying nothing but a 99-cent pair of men's socks. "Look at what *they* get, and look at all *I* get," he'd say to the clerk with a "poor me" expression.

Dad didn't have to be me, either. Sometimes, I'd call him from a store at the mall and plead, "They're having this great sale, dad."

"Put the sales clerk on the phone," he'd respond, heroically. Then he'd proceed to give the clerk his credit card number. "Make sure she gets whatever she wants," he'd threaten. "In fact, I want you to help her max out my credit card or I'll never let her shop at your store again!"

One summer, I was on a YMCA trip to Canada with a bus load of other kids. Heavy rains had ruined not only our camping plans, but our food, as well. We were all quite frustrated and very hungry. "Hey, I think my dad has a connection with a restaurant somewhere in Canada," I thought out loud. I went to the nearest telephone and called Dad collect.

"Stay right there by the telephone, Sheri Rose." he said. Within the next ten minutes, my father had arranged for all 100 of us dirty little campers to eat free-of-charge at one of the fanciest restaurants in the area. The owner even agreed to close the restaurant's doors from five to seven p.m. to allow us kids to stampede in and munch out on steak and lobster dinner! I immediately became the most popular kid at the YMCA, thanks to Dad's single-handed rescue.

Dad told me he got the knack for getting things done from his mother, grandma Sadie. Once, she wanted to speak with her eldest son Kent real bad (you know how mom's are!). Well, unfortunately, Kent was somewhere in the jungle in the Philippines during World War II! That didn't stop her. She spent a solid week on the phone hopping around from the Red Cross to every platoon in the United States Army until she finally tracked him down in a foxhole!

"Are you Kent Goodman?"

"Yeah. Why?"

"Well, your mom's on the phone and she's really worried about you."

Like Grandma Sadie, patience, was never one of my dad's virtues. I remember once, my dad and I were in line at the grocery store behind some people who were taking forever questioning the bill and putzing around with their checkbook. After a few minutes, my dad had reached his limit. Next thing you know, in one giant swoop, he ripped the checkbook from their hand, threw some cash down and shouted, "Here's the money. Now get the #$@&*! out of the way. I'm in a hurry!"

In restaurants, my Dad would often say to the server, "We feel like being obnoxious tonight, so if you can do everything we ask you to and put up with us, I'll tip you the entire amount of the bill." Needless to say, our bill was usually pretty huge by the time we were done. Dad would hear us trying to decide which appetizer to get, and he'd say

"Why work so hard to pick something? We'll just get *all* of them!" He'd then turn to the server and say, "Tell you what— we'll have two of every appetizer on the menu, and what we don't finish, throw in the ocean for good luck!"

Chapter 5

The Power of Words

When my dad wasn't stressed-out, he could be a very positive person. He'd often go out of his way to encourage people and make them feel special. I remember times we'd be dining out (which was quite often), and he'd grab a busboy's arm and say to him, "Remember, son, you can be anything you want to be. Don't ever let anyone tell you any different." I could see a young man's face change right before my eyes—they'd beam, they'd stand a little taller. To this day, I still hear from people who tell me, "Sheri, you have no idea the impact your dad had on my success." Dad truly understood the incredible power of words.

As a depressed, unattractive, overweight child, it was tough for me to endure the vicious words spoken to me by other kids. I remember one particular lunch time at school when I was being teased and called "Fatty". I started to cry. A teacher, having seen it all, came up to me and scolded, "You're such a baby. No wonder they make fun of you." I was devastated. I locked myself in a stall in the bathroom and cried until all the kids were off the playground. Teachers have an incredible effect on their students. I remember practically nothing from my early years in school. All my grade school memories seem to melt together into one giant, dark cloud of pain and loneliness.

One thing I do remember is my fourth-grade teacher, Mr.

Hagwood—a warm, tender man who would laugh with us and sing songs to us. When Mr. Hagwood saw me getting teased about being 'fat' and 'stupid', he offered comfort. "Don't pay attention to what those kids say. Someday you're going to grow up to be something great." I'll bet you can guess that I loved Mr. Hagwood dearly. I wanted to do well for him, and I worked hard and got my usual 'C' and 'D' level grades up to a 'B'. I was so proud! Thanks to the encouragement of dear Mr. Hagwood.

I failed at almost every sport or activity I ever attempted because no one believed in me, including myself. Words of encouragement can be so powerful. Once, my dad took me to an ice rink in Squaw Valley where I watched the graceful skaters on the ice.

"Dad, I want to try!" I said excitedly. At last, something was sparking my interest.

"You could be as good or better than anyone out there if you wanted to, Sheri," he told me encouragingly.

I put on a rented pair of ice skates. Remembering Dad's words, I wanted to prove to him that he was right and to my surprise, I did pretty well. I started going faster and faster and with a huge smile, I yelled, "Dad! Look at me! I'm doing it!" Just as I began to feel confident, I crashed head on, right into an ice skating coach and knocked him and myself on our rear ends.

"Have you ever skated before?" he asked, as he helped me to my feet.

"This is my first time, ever," I replied.

"I'd love to teach you some basics. You have the natural talent to become very good," he said.

Dad signed me up for lessons immediately. I found out

later that this wasn't just any coach, but he was one of Peggy Fleming's coaches! I couldn't wait to start learning.

I kept up with my skating, and loved every minute of it until my parents divorced. I then reluctantly hung up my skates and continued with my second favorite thing—eating. Oh, how I wish I had stuck with it. Skating, that is! To this day, I dream about gliding gracefully across the ice— effortlessly executing flawless double axles, triple-toe loops, and sit spins!

Chapter 6

Breaking Up is Hard To Do

By the time I was eight or nine years-old, my parents' fighting had reached such a violent intensity that it was becoming unbearable. I actually began to beg them, "Just get a divorce. I don't want you to be together anymore. All you do is fight!" Years later, my dad told me he would have divorced at that point, if it weren't for my brother Michael and me.

It was in 1973, when I was in the sixth grade, that it finally happened. On New Years Eve '72, my father was home alone. My mother had taken me and Michael to Lake Tahoe and a neighbor girl came to the house and told Dad that my mom had been having an affair for the last five years with one of the doctors from the hospital. My dad decided that was the final straw. The next day, January 2, 1973, he filed for divorce.

When we got home from Tahoe, Mom and Dad had their last fight. "You can marry this guy," Dad conceded, "I give up." He then packed some things, walked out, and moved into an apartment down the street. In court, he told Mom, "You can have everything. I don't want to fight anymore. I just want the kids to be taken care of."

Dad was so embarrassed in front of his coworkers about the divorce, that he decided to take a job in San Jose selling ads for a new magazine. Unfortunately, little did he suspect, but there was no magazine after all. It was a "front", a scam. The people who hired him took the money and ran. Well, hitting a brick wall like that never stopped my father before. He picked up the pieces and started his own advertising agency.

Michael and I flew to San Jose every other weekend to see our dad. Early on, he asked us to make a pact with him to never bring up Mom. I noticed one dramatic change in him right away. He didn't seem to be be having any of his "blow-ups". Not anymore.

Mom had a tough time after the divorce. The doctor she'd been seeing over the years broke up with her and went back to his wife. She lost the few friends she had. Then, even though finances were not a problem, she started getting paranoid about the future. She began taking extremely frugal measures like buying us nothing but second-hand clothes. Next, she decided to sell the house to save money for her future, and we moved into a smaller place in a dumpy neighborhood.

Our move meant I'd have to switch to a new school as I started seventh grade. But, even though I was the "new kid" again, I was feeling very optimistic—like I had a chance for a fresh start. This attitude helped me find comfort in food a bit less frequently. I'd been quite overweight for the last few years, so the little bit of weight I lost really made me feel like I was making progress. What I felt I really needed most were friends.

I was always very outgoing, but it seemed like only the "druggies" were accepting of me. Maybe it's because they were pretty laid back most of the time or, because so many of them came from dysfunctional families like mine. It may have had something to do with the fact that I had started drinking and was still smoking pot regularly. In any case, I developed some friendships among this group.

I also began to discover some other ways to increase my popularity. The first way was by using my father's money to buy lunches, treats, and presents for the other kids. It always worked for my dad— he always seemed to save the day and win friends. Suddenly, I had some new found popularity.

To keep this popularity, I found myself caving in to peer pressure. Once, some of my so-called friends pressured me to shoplift a pack of cigarettes from a store. "It's easy," they taunted. "C'mon! Go get us some." So I did. Next thing I knew, I was being handcuffed and taken to Juvenile Hall. Fortunately, the counselor there was a friend of my dad's. Even though I got off easy with the LAW, I sat nervously as the counselor made the dreaded call to my Dad, who then drove down from San Jose to pick me up. I was scared to death of what he might say or do to me. He walked in and saw me, put his hand on my shoulder and said, "C'mon, let's go eat." I was astounded and relieved. As we talked, he didn't dwell long on what I had done. He simply admonished me not to do it again. "You're too good to get involved with kids like that," he added.

As eighth grade began, I developed a huge crush on a boy named Keith. I got word that he had said to someone, "Sheri would be really pretty if she just lost some weight." My heart jumped in my chest! I was determined to lose another 10 to 15 pounds so, I stopped pigging out like I was so used to doing. The day after I got my braces off, I bumped into Keith in the school office. I grinned from ear to ear to show off my new and improved smile, and immediately struck up a conversation with this adorable boy. He had just gotten his braces off too! One thing led to another, and Keith and I started going steady.

I started spending a lot of time at Keith's house. Besides wanting to be near Keith, there were other reasons. Keith lived in a "richer", nicer neighborhood than I did, and his parents, who were Christians, treated me wonderfully. My home life was still pretty depressing, so I thought of every reason I could to head to his place, and, to keep from leaving. Of course, my mom became quite jealous of my relationship with Keith's family.

Thanks to my new outlook on life, my new relationship, and my new surrogate family, I even began to get better grades. Even a few A's here and there! But when my mother saw the A's, she accused me of cheating to get them. I was crushed. Her words killed my desire to ever do well in school again.

Then, toward the end of the school year, Keith fell for someone else. While we were together, he had pressured me constantly to have sex, but I wasn't ready. I guess his new girlfriend would give him what he wanted. I was devastated, and missed Keith terribly. I vividly remember that, whenever I saw him at school with his new girlfriend, I either ran to the field across from school to get "high" with the druggies or I helped myself to double portions of junk food at the snack bar. I thought about his house and his parents and dreaded going home to my miserable family.

The day Keith and I broke up, I came home to find that my mother had taken Michael to Lake Tahoe with her, leaving me behind. I found a note telling me where they'd gone with an explanation tacked on, "After all, you don't really want to be with us anyway." (Which was true, partly because I resented

29

how close the two of them were). When they came back, they made sure I knew what a great time they had together.

While they were gone, I occupied part of the time by snooping around in my mom's room. It was then that I found records showing how much money Mom was getting from Dad. She'd been telling us all along how Dad wasn't paying enough, and how much we had to suffer because of him. Now I realized that she wasn't telling the truth, and I practically hit the ceiling. Not only did I resent her actions, I was hurt that she would deprive us and then blame dad. At age 14, it was legal for me to choose which parent to live with, so, I decided to call my dad to tell him I wanted to move in with him.

Dad arranged for me to fly to San Jose. When he picked me up, he could see I'd been crying (so what else was new?), and I looked terrible. He told me we had to stop for a business meeting at one of the radio stations and suggested that I'd better wait out in the lobby for just a little while. He'd only been gone a few minutes when my tears started up again. This attracted the attention of one of the women who worked at the station. "Hi, I'm Denise. What's wrong, sweetie? Are you okay?" Between sobs, I managed to answer her questions. It turned out she was a friend of Dad's. "Let me take you to lunch," she offered. By this time, I was feeling quite comfortable with her so I eagerly accepted. She got an OK from my dad, and over lunch, I told her my whole story.

Denise was a pleasant, compassionate woman in her mid-thirties who seemed to understand me. She was no stranger to broken-home situations herself—she'd been divorced, and her eight year-old daughter was living with her ex-husband. After hearing my story, she made me an incredible offer, "I really want to help you. Why don't you move in with me?" We talked it over with Dad, and he agreed.

Naturally, Mom was devastated by my choice to move out. She was even more irate when she found out I was moving in with a substitute mother. At one point, she told me, "No one has ever hurt me more than you have!" I felt, since we seemed to hurt each other so much when we were together, we would probably be better off apart.

Even though my relationship with Mom had taken a downward turn, I felt like I had a real chance for a fresh start staying with my new friend Denise. I enrolled in high school in San Jose, and really liked it at first, but then I made the mistake of bonding with the druggies again. I couldn't manage to find the strength to quit smoking marijuana, even though I wanted to. It was my security blanket, and sometimes it seemed that everyone around me smoked pot, too. Denise wasn't any help at all—even she smoke it! I had no motivation or self-discipline, so my over-eating continued to be a serious problem— I gained over 30 pounds.

Chapter 7

Dad, You Don't Have a Choice!

Occasionally, Dad's work would require him to return to Sacramento where Mom and Michael lived. More often than not, I'd accompany him on these trips. We'd stay in a nice hotel and my brother Michael would come over and stay with us.

On one particular trip, we were staying at the Woodlake Inn. I heard Dad comment about Susie, a cocktail waitress in the hotel bar, "She's really nice. And a real knockout, too." That's all the encouragement I needed. I decided to play matchmaker. While Dad, Michael, and I were down at the hotel pool, I took the opportunity to sneak off and pay Susie a visit. She was a beautiful brunette with a contagious laugh and a gorgeous body. My eyes lit up as I pulled up a bar stool and got her attention.

"Would you go out with my dad?" I asked. (Hey, why beat around the bush?)

"Oh, I might," she responded, half-way holding back a laugh.

"Is that a yes or a no?"

"Well.... yes. Maybe."

"So that's a yes, right?" I slammed down my fist, vaulted from the stool, ran out of the bar and yelled across the pool, "Hey, Dad! Susie said she'd go out with you! ...and you're right! She *is* a knockout!" I looked around and realized I had drawn the attention of virtually everyone in the vicinity. To this day, Dad reminds me of how I provided him with one of his life's most embarrassing moments.

I then realized that I'd better go back in and make sure I closed the deal.

"Okay, when?" I implored Susie.

"Errr...I guess tonight's alright," Susie laughed. I spun on my heels and dashed back to the pool with the news.

All the way back to our hotel room, Michael and I begged Dad to go through with it, but he kept resisting us. "I promised this would be *our* weekend," he protested, "I told you we'd spend it together doing anything you kids wanted."

I realized we'd have to adjust our strategy slightly, "Okay, Dad. You're right. So you said you'll do whatever we want, right?"

"Right."

"Then what we want is for you to go out with Susie tonight," Michael and I nodded in agreement.

He could tell we weren't going to give in, so he went. He had a great time and Michael and I practically jumped him when he walked through the door, "We want you to marry her, Dad!"

"That was just our first date!" he objected. But our minds were made up.

After returning to San Jose, Dad kept in touch with Susie by phone, and would fly her up to be with him on the occasional weekend. Dad wasn't completely sold on this long distance relationship idea, though, and continued dating other women. Or, at least he tried. I absolutely would not accept any of the other women he brought around, and went so far as to refuse to acknowledge their presence. I was such a stinker!

It was during this period that Dad bought a large house across the street from his office for Denise and me to move into. He kept his apartment, though, and continued to live there. This arrangement went on for about nine months when things began changing rapidly.

Denise fell in love with the man she'd been dating and Dad's relationship with Susie began to heat up. So, out went Denise, and in moved Dad and Susie, and, eventually Susie's 14 year-old son, Lanny, whom I adored.

After a few months, Dad was ready to propose. He took Susie out to a nice restaurant for a romantic dinner on the patio. Toward the end of the meal, he pointed skyward pretending to be surprised, "What the heck is that?" Susie looked up to see the blimp my dad had hired to spell out his "love note" in the sky. She cried as she read the heavenly phrases such as 'I love you,' 'I can't live without you,' and, of course, 'Will you marry me?' Dad produced a ring that was so big, it's a wonder Susie didn't need an arm sling to help keep it up. Her answer was yes.

My brother Michael began to visit our new "family" a lot more often now. He preferred the way it felt to be part of a real family, and he loved hanging out with our new step-brother, Lanny. It also didn't hurt that we lived in a nice house surrounded by nice things. Susie wasn't a stern, bossy mother—she was so "cool" it was like having another good friend around. The lure of all this proved to be too over-whelming for young Michael, and he informed our mother that he, too, wanted to live with Dad. This was yet another in a series of crushing blows dealt to Mom.

As Michael prepared to move in, Dad informed the rest of us that since he hadn't had Michael for so long, he intended to spoil him for awhile. Did he ever! No matter the situation, whatever Michael wanted, Michael got. We went where Michael wanted to go, we did what Michael wanted to do. Everyone else's suggestions or requests were always overridden. This went on for so long that Susie, Lanny, and I developed some major resentment over it. It took no time at all for Michael to realize that he had incredible power in his new family and he started to abuse it.

Soon, the one thing I'd been most apprehensive about in moving in with my dad—his temper—began to resurface. Dad was trying so hard to overcompensate for Michael, that he forgot about the rest of the family and it caused a lot of tension. Dad also became extremely possessive of me. Any boy I liked, he hated. He was also jealous of my friends. He'd often explode when he thought I was spending too much time with them. He saw it as "protecting" me—I saw it as a prison. Naturally, I wanted to break out. Then there was the time I made the mistake of borrowing his hallowed hairbrush. I used it, then stuck it in my purse and went off to a party at a friend's house. My dad discovered what I'd done, and was so furious that he immediately drove over to the party to confront me. There I was in front of all the other kids, with my father screaming at me and practically foaming at the mouth over a stupid hairbrush! I was more than humiliated. He really scared me when he was like this. I continued to turn to pot to escape from the pain and fear, but it always seemed to be a losing battle. The more pot I smoked, the more I ate. That year brought me more anxiety— and another twenty pounds.

Chapter 8

Out of Control!

During the second semester of my junior year, at the urging of a guidance counselor, I decided to enroll in a program that would allow me to attend beauty school for half of each school day. Although I did poorly on the book work, I did very well at the actual "hands-on" stuff— make-up application, hair styling, etc. I seemed to have a natural gift to make people beautiful. Maybe it was because I wanted so badly to be beautiful myself.

Of course, my first "client" may not have been so quick to agree with this assessment. Some women in the neighborhood would come to the school to have their hair done, knowing that because we were students, the rates would be very inexpensive. When my turn came to work on one of these ladies, I took her over to the shampoo basin and had her lean her head back onto the headrest. I accidentally turned the faucet on so hard that the water hit the bottom of the basin, shot back up in the air and drenched the poor woman's face! I frantically grabbed for the nearest towel and proceeded to wipe off her false eyelashes and fake eyebrows! I looked at the smudged towel, then looked at her face. I tried to control myself but couldn't. I suddenly exploded into a fit of hysterical laughter. I then ran into the bathroom to hide until I could get control of myself.

With this incident behind me, I went on to become a top

student at beauty school. After doing quite a few successful makeovers, word of my newfound talents began to spread among the other girls in high school. Soon, I was the most "booked" of all the beauty school students. It was a mixed blessing for me though, because week after week I made other girls look fabulous for their dates while week after week I sat home alone. It didn't seem fair. But, who wanted to date someone as overweight as I was? No one, it seemed.

One night, I had just come home after being out late with some friends. As I walked to my room, I could hear Michael and Lanny carrying on in one of the other rooms, laughing uproariously—obviously stoned. They didn't know I was there, so I listened to see what they found so funny. They were talking into a tape recorder, pretending to be disc jockeys.

"Who should we interview?" I heard them say.

"Let's interview, Sheri the Whale!"

"Yes, here she comes, it's Sheri the Whale. She walks like a penguin, but she looks like a whale. If I were as big as her, I'd play for the 49ers!"

"No. If you were as big as her, you'd be the entire team!"

As painful as it is to be teased about your weight, the pain is never greater than when it comes from the people you care most about—from your own family—a pain so intense, you'd do almost anything not to feel it anymore.

I turned once again to the one thing that consistently seemed to take my pain away—Marijuana. Soon, I was getting stoned morning, noon, and night. Every day at school, I'd be sitting in class high as a kite. Then, for no apparent reason, I'd just start crying and couldn't stop. I'd then have to excuse myself to the restroom, or, as often happened, I'd be sent to the counselor's office. Fortunately, my counselor was a very caring man who would listen to me compassionately for hours, but, that didn't help me get away from dope. In fact, I soon began to experiment with other kinds of drugs.

Once at lunch, my friends and I put a hallucinogen known as "Magic Mushrooms" in our burgers. My next class was English with Mrs. Pace, a round-faced woman with short brown hair who was easily provoked. Halfway through the class, it quickly became obvious to her that I was in no shape to learn English or any other subject. "You'll never amount to anything," she pronounced, staring at me with utter disgust. I, however, was too far gone to let it bother me.

I started to hallucinate, imagining I could see little things flying around her and landing on her. I was giddy by now. I leaned to a friend, and yelled the loudest whisper I'm sure the class had ever heard, "Psssssst! Hey, Karen! Look at all those flies diving at Mrs. Pace!" The class roared in laughter as Mrs. Pace closed in. She hovered over me like a vulture— her head spinning with anger. She took a controlled breath and grumbled, "Do you have some sort of problem, Sheri Rose?" I responded by whacking an imaginary fly on the top of her head! She sent me straight to the principal's office and, naturally, I was suspended from school. Yes, Mrs. Pace, I *did* have a problem!

A new family start! That's Me, Michael, Stepmom Susie, Dad, and new brother, Lanny.

We went to lots of concerts in Lake Tahoe. Here we are before the Osmond's Show.

I used to get stoned every day as a freshman...before and after school.

Chapter 9

An Independent Dependent

It amazes me that my Dad had no idea how bad his daughter's drug problem really was. Of course, he was too stressed out to deal with it anyway, and, he simply continued his outrageous style of living.

His advertising agency really started to take off, and he was making more money than ever, so he decided to purchase a much bigger house for us. He also decided that each one of us kids should have our own personal interior decorator to design our bedrooms. I'll never forget the conversation he had with the decorator he hired to do the main parts of the house.

"I want you to find me three other decorators to do each of the kids' rooms," Dad instructed.

"Well, Mr. Goodman, you know, it would be my pleasure to do the entire job."

"No, I want them each to have their own."

"Well, I'd be delighted to work with your children, and I can easily handle the whole job, really I can."

"What I want you to *handle* is finding me three more decorators! Now shut up, lose the battle, and win the war!" As usual, Dad got his way.

Lanny's room was an ocean theme, complete with an underwater mural that covered three walls. Michael's mural was a breathtaking vision of a snowy white Lake Tahoe during ski season. I had a gorgeous Yosemite Park mural complete with a working model waterfall, a king-sized, four-poster brass waterbed and a real sheepskin bedspread.

As much difficulty as I had with my dad's temper, I knew that deep down inside, he loved me and wanted the best for me. Maybe that's why he overdid it with the "hero" image. Once at school, "that time of the month" arrived, and I was without any feminine napkins. I was too embarrassed to ask anyone else, so I phoned my dad. He canceled a very important business meeting and galloped to the rescue with a box of Tampax, Midol, bottled water, and some chocolates! The Lone Ranger to the rescue!

On another occasion, I mentioned to my dad about my driver's education class and how rude the football coach was who taught it. He treated everyone badly, was especially mean to the girls and that particular day, was being exceptionally nasty to me right in front of the class. The next day, I was astonished to see my dad march right into my class and tell the teacher off. I was humiliated and embarrassed! I must admit, however, that my teacher was noticeably kinder from that day on.

These "rescues" were certainly giving me a rather warped view of how to get along in the world. But at age 16, as happens with many teenage girls, I began yearning to discover what it would feel like to be more independent. Even though we certainly didn't need the money, I decided to try my hand at a part-time job. I wanted the fun and experience of working and earning some extra cash on my own.

I waltzed right in to a restaurant called the Velvet Turtle and asked about a waitressing job. As it turned out, my timing was perfect because one of their waitresses had just quit, leaving them shorthanded. "How old are you?" the manager asked me.

"Errr...I'm 18," I lied.

"And you have experience?"

"Oh sure!" I lied some more.

"You've handled heavy trays?"

"No problem," I assured him.

"Great. You can start tonight!"

Of course, I had never held a tray in my life. So, on my very first order, I emerged from the kitchen with two spinach salads, and promptly dumped them, tray and all, on top of a man's head. Then I proceeded to compound the matter by laughing at my handiwork. When the manager came out and spotted me laughing my head off while picking spinach leaves off this poor man's lap, he fired me on the spot. So much for independence!

One other time I had a job that a compulsive-eating teen would die for. For three months, I was an under-cover restaurant spy for *Der Weinerschnitzel*. A manager would drop me off at six or seven of their stores three nights a week while I posed as a customer. I ate french-fries and chili cheese dogs four times per night as I snooped around and checked out the employees. The money was nice, but, with a job like that, I did far more than just *pad* my pockets!

Chapter 10

A Whale of A Prom!

I'm sure all teenage girls fantasize about going to the prom with their dream date and having an unforgettably magical night. As a high school junior carrying around 50 extra pounds, I had no delusions about being swept off to the prom by a handsome prince. I was quite sure that no one would even ask me, and I was right. I did throw some major hints at a few guys, but they all gave me the "friends" speech or found other ways to squirm away.

I tried not to let it get to me, but as the prom neared, I started to feel like the only girl in the junior class who hadn't been asked. And, to add insult to injury, a lot of girls were begging me to do their make-up and hair for the occasion.

I couldn't take it any longer. About a week before the prom, I approached my friend Marlene with an idea. "Marlene, I want to go to the prom so bad. Do you think, if I paid for everything, your brother Ron would take me?" She thought there was enough of a chance to make it worth asking, so we went to her house to pop the question.

Ron was in his room getting stoned when I walked in. "Hey, Ron, I was wondering...are you going to the prom?"

"Nahhh. I don't really wanna go."

"Would you go with me if I paid for everything?"

"Well...I guess if we went, like, as part of a group of

people...then, yeah, I guess so." Sure, I know his heart wasn't really in it, but I didn't care at the time. I was going to the prom after all.

My stepmom Susie was thrilled and said she'd take me to get a prom dress. Dad offered up a credit card as his contribution, and Susie and I headed for the mall. Susie was aghast, though, when I selected a brightly-colored, sleeveless, polyester, floral-print dress. "Sheri, no. Listen to me, honey, you want to stick with dark colors and sleeves. Otherwise, you'll look too...well, too heavy." I wasn't persuaded however, so she persisted, "Trust me, sweetie, if you wear this, you'll look at your prom pictures when you get them, and you'll really regret it." But I had made up my mind.

Susie then tried to steer me toward some nice, feminine shoes. I rejected them and chose, of all things, a pair of rubber thongs! "Look how well the color goes with the dress," I insisted. Realizing she couldn't talk me out of my choices, Susie reluctantly conceded.

Prom night arrived, and Ron and me and three other couples went together. Of course, we all got stoned first. The dinner was nice enough, then the dancing began. I wanted to dance with Ron, but he wouldn't. He said he didn't like dancing. So, there I sat. Maybe a miracle would happen and someone else would ask me. A little later in the evening, my heart jumped into my throat when a guy I had a big crush on approached me. "Hey, Sheri, are you going to the beach?" he inquired.

I thought maybe he meant that some of the kids were going to head for the beach after the dance. "Why, are you?" I responded.

"No," came his reply, "I just thought you were going to

the beach 'cause you look like a whale and you're wearing thongs!" I realized that this evening was definitely not turning out as planned.

Then came the time for pictures to be taken. I got in line with a reluctant Ron, and when it was our turn, Ron joked with the photographer, "Are you sure you can fit me in the picture with her?"

So all-in-all, a pretty romantic night—having to pay the brother of a friend to take me to my prom to sit and watch everyone else have fun. At the time, I didn't see how things could get any worse. But they did.

Chapter 11

Surprise, Surprise!

On my seventeenth birthday, my dad, the guy who does everything big, decided to throw me a party I'd never forget. He rented a stable, hired a live band, provided enough barbecued filet mignon for an army, and furnished unlimited draft beer to everyone who came. We had flyers printed up and distributed all around school. About 150 kids came to the stables for a night of eating, drinking, dancing, hayrides, and more.

I was dancing with a few of my girlfriends when one of the guys came up to me holding two cups of beer. "Here, I have a surprise birthday present for you," he said, offering me one of the cups. I thought it was a really sweet gesture, and I gave him a hug for it.

"C'mon let's chug 'em," he urged. So we did. "We're going on a trip tonight," he laughed.

"Really? Where? To the beach?" I asked naively.

"Oh you'll see," he grinned, and went off to dance with someone.

About an hour after drinking the beer, I had gone to the bathroom, and was just about to emerge, when I began to hallucinate. The bathroom was suddenly filled with the sound of this horrible, maniacal laughter. It sounded like an entire crowd of people laughing at me and taunting me. I looked up to see what was happening and the ceiling appeared to be completely covered with hundreds of distorted, evil-looking faces staring down at me.

I screamed and stumbled outside to my friends. The faces followed me. Laughing...taunting. I managed to find the so-called friend who gave me the beer. "What was in that drink?", I yelled frantically.

"Sugar-cube acid," came his answer, proudly. His surprise birthday gift to me was a horrendous trip on LSD.

"How can I stop it? Give me something to get rid of it!" I screamed. But there was nothing he could do. I suddenly felt like my body was floating upward toward the faces. "Help me, please! Hold on to me, don't let them touch me! God, please don't let them get me!" I gripped at the air in desperate fear.

"Come with me," he said, and took me to his VW van. I got inside, but the faces continued to follow me, howling with laughter and screaming. We drove off, but there was no escape. Eventually, he had to take me home.

I wanted desperately for this nightmare to end, but it wouldn't. I was haunted by the menacing evil of this dreadful "acid trip" for three days. I refused to let my parents take me to the hospital. I wouldn't eat, I couldn't sleep. I just floated, frantically scratching and clawing for something real, something safe. No one could help me. I just had to wait it out.

On the third day, the horror ceased. I found myself on the floor of my bathroom, crying. I slowly pulled myself up to the mirror. What I saw was very strange. It seemed as though I was seeing myself clearly for the first time in my life. I knew then that I had to change—to get off this nightmarish road to destruction. I knew I needed help, but I didn't know where to turn. My mother hadn't spoken to me since I had moved out,

47

and Dad's too busy, I thought, groping for a solution. I was also just too afraid to tell him that his daughter was a complete loser.

Just when I thought I had run out of hope, my stepmom, Susie, opened the door and asked, "Are you alright?" I ran into her arms and cried, "I hate my life! Please help me!" Susie herself had overcome many obstacles and challenges in her life, and when anyone around her was falling apart, she was a pillar of strength. She had been waiting for me to ask.

She led me out of the bathroom, sat me down on the edge of the bed, gently comforting me. She encouraged me to take responsibility for myself. "You can only blame your parents and hide behind your drugs for so long," she said. "I've always wanted to say these things to you, but your dad wouldn't let me. He thought I'd upset you and drive a wedge between us." She proceeded to share her own story with me and made me feel that, if she could make it, I could make it too.

Then she offered to help me. But only under *her* conditions. She said I'd have to give up the things that were destroying my life—my friends, my wild weekends, my sugar fixes, my drug use, my cigarettes—all of it. She told me she'd pick me up every day after school, work out with me, cook me healthy meals, and be my best friend.

I'd always admired Susie, so I was excited about having her by my side, helping me make these positive changes. She was true to her word, too. She did all the things she said she would, and then some. She went for walks with me, took me to lunch, took me shopping, laughed with me, and so much more. I knew it wasn't going to be easy to stick to the new standard of living she'd set for me, but I was so desperate to change my life's direction that I made a covenant with her that I would try my very best.

This is the photo my Stepmom Susie taped up on the refrigerator. I couldn't believe this was actually me.

The famous blue floral polyester prom dress worn with rubber thongs. I paid for his tux, too.

Chapter 12

A New Start!

I remember quite clearly the first morning of my "new start". I wondered what it would be like to go to school and not smoke a cigarette or a joint, and to have lunch without pizza, french fries, or twinkies. It was going to be torture, I thought. My stepmom drove me to school. "Be strong. You can do it," she encouraged me. I knew I had a lot of challenges in front of me—facing old friends, old habits, and my old self. I made it through that first day, and felt a small victory.

Later that week, my dad signed me up at a health club across the street from my highschool in San Jose. The club manager took my measurements and weighed me in. I tipped the scales at 175 pounds and reached 5' 4" in height. When he asked me why I wanted to join, I sarcastically quipped, "I'm going to be the next Miss USA!" He just smiled and said I had a great sense of humor. This reminded me of what friends tell you when you ask them if the blind date they want to fix you up with is cute…"Well, he has a great sense of humor," they'll say. I decided a long time ago that 'a great sense of humor' must be code words for 'fat or ugly'. Well, no matter. Every day after school, I faithfully walked over to the club and worked out.

By the end of the summer of 1978, I was on my way to accomplishing goals I never would have believed I could reach.

I'd lost 40 pounds, quit smoking and drinking, and stuck to the rules my stepmother had set for me. Honestly though, I don't think I could have conquered these obstacles in my life if I hadn't kept my eyes firmly on my goal, and if I hadn't had someone to hold me accountable.

Chapter 13

Prince Running-Back

My senior year—what a difference! I had changed everything about myself—my habits, my friends, my wardrobe, my hair color, my weight, (I even grew two inches taller!) and most importantly, my attitude.

My new routine included running around the track at the highschool after my workout at the health club. One afternoon during my run, I heard a voice from behind me, "Get your knees higher!" I kept running—surely it wasn't meant for me, I thought. But again the voice came, only louder this time, "Get your knees up!"

I turned to see a handsome young man approach, smiling at me. "Why are you yelling at me?" I asked, defensively.

"Because you want to be the next Miss USA, don't you?"

"Where did you get that idea?" I shot back.

"Remember when you stepped up on the scale at the health club that first day? I was standing behind you. I've watched you work hard toward your goal for the past nine months, and I'm proud of you." My guard immediately dropped.

Proud of me? I couldn't remember when anyone other than my father or Susie had ever been proud of me for anything. The young man's name was Marc Rebboah, a sophomore at the University of Santa Clara. "I want to train you for the

Miss California Pageant coming up," he continued. "With my help, I really think you can win."

I thought I was dreaming. I wasn't used to having handsome strangers telling me they believed in me and offering to help me reach a personal goal. And anyway, I was still pretty unsure of myself. My dad had taken me to dozens of pageants when he was a disc jockey and I always fantasized about the perfect smiles, the shapely bodies, and the radiance of a thousand lights.

"Miss California? Me? Is he talking to the right girl?" I thought. He then assured me that he'd teach me everything I needed to know. I kept thinking there must be a catch. Someone's probably playing a cruel joke on me.

"We'll start meeting at the gym every day after school," he explained. "You'll have to work out at least two hours every day. Then we'll go over the latest newspapers and magazines, 'cause you'll have to be up on current events if you expect to win a pageant."

After a few weeks of this, I realized that this guy was for real, and I was really starting to fall for him, but my insecurities stopped me short. "Someone like *him* with some-one like *me*? No way," I thought. We were just too different. I couldn't read or write very well—he was a 4.0 college student. I'd abused drugs and alcohol—he was as straight as they come, never smoked a cigarette or a joint and never had a drink in his life. He could speak two languages—I was barely coherent with just English. He was a history major—I didn't know much about the *present* state of the world, let alone the past. He was drop-dead gorgeous—I still saw myself as fat and ugly.

Nevertheless, I began to think about Marc so much that I could barely focus on anything else. So, when my friend

Karen suggested we go dancing at an under-age dance club, I thought it would be just the thing to take my mind off Marc for awhile.

I needed Karen's help with my clothes and make-up. Sure, I could do great work helping other girls in this area, but I still had a real block when it came to doing it for myself—I guess I couldn't yet believe that any combination of clothes and make-up could ever make me beautiful. Karen did a fabulous job on my make-up, put a flower in my hair, and gave me some really dynamite wrap-around pants to wear. (I couldn't believe that I actually fit into her Size 3 clothes!) We told my dad we were going to the movies and then would spend the night at Karen's—he'd never have let me go to a dance club.

From the very moment we walked in, I was stunned to see how much attention I was getting from guys as I walked past (no rubber thongs, this time!). I was having trouble believing that boys found me attractive, and I said as much to Karen. "Believe it, girl," she said. "You're beautiful!"

This is a real turning point in my life, I thought, as we danced into the night. I felt like Cinderella at the Ball. The only thing missing was the Prince. At that moment, I looked up to see a familiar face looking back at me from across the dance floor. It was Marc!

I couldn't believe this was really happening. We went outside to talk. "You are *so* gorgeous," he said as I blushed. At the end of the night, do I get to keep the flower in your hair?"

"Why do you want it?" I asked.

"Because I want to remember this night forever," he replied. Maybe this was a fairy tale after all.

"So what are you doing here tonight?" I inquired. You

have to be under 20 to get in."

"I used my brother's ID," he explained, "I knew you'd be here."

I was curious to know how he knew. Right about then, one of his friends saw him and commented, "What are you doing hanging around with a druggie, Marc?" I know for a fact he took a lot of grief for the time he spent with me. People couldn't understand why he'd want to associate with such a "loser". But he ignored them all.

"Someday," he told me, "you'll put everybody to shame for everything they ever said or thought about you." How did this guy always know just the right thing to say?

Marc and I stayed out quite late talking, and Karen had gone back to her house ahead of me. When Marc and I finally arrived at Karen's, we found out that my dad had called Karen's and panicked when I wasn't there. He even had the police out scouring the town for me. Marc drove me home to face the music. I was terrified at what my dad would do to me, but after the evening I'd had, I thought, "whatever he does to me, it's worth it."

I walked in the house and, before my father could utter a word, I said, "Dad, I don't care what you do to me. You can punish me, or whatever you want, because tonight I met the man I'm going to marry." I don't know if it was what I said, or the way I said it, but it worked. Instead of exploding, he was totally taken aback.

"Well, who is this guy?" Dad finally said.

"His name is Marc Rebboah."

Michael and Lanny, who had no doubt stayed up to see me "get it" from Dad, both exclaimed, "Marc Rebboah! *The* Marc Rebboah?? Yeah, right. Get real." I assured them I was telling the truth, but they stared at one another dumfounded. "It *can't* be the same one," they protested.

"What do you mean? How do you guys know who he is?" I asked.

Dad retrieved a local newspaper and handed it to me. There, on the front page, was a picture of Marc! "He's the star running back for Santa Clara's football team and he's already been approached by the Dallas Cowboys," one of them explained. "You've been hanging around with Marc Rebboah for two months and you didn't know all this?" I had to admit I didn't. Marc hadn't told me anything about his local fame.

"Let's have him over sometime soon," said Dad.

"This is amazing," I thought. "Not only was I *not* in trouble, it seemed I had suddenly attained celebrity status". Speaking the name 'Marc Rebboah' was like some kind of magic charm.

Lanny and Michael, however, were quick to add, "There's no way he'll ever want someone like *you* for a girlfriend." I cried myself to sleep that night, wondering if their cruel words would prove true.

By the following afternoon, I was convinced Lanny and Michael were right, and I was determined not to set myself up for disappointment. When Marc arrived at the gym, I told him, "I don't want to work out with you anymore." I tried to walk away, but he grabbed my arm.

"What the heck are you talking about?" he demanded. I resisted telling him at first, but finally opened up to him. I told him I knew who he really was and pointed out all the differences between us—all the reasons why it made no sense for us to be together. He just smiled at me and said, "That's one of the reasons why I like you so much, because you liked me even though you didn't know who I was. And, you're *not* like other girls. You work harder to reach your goals and to improve yourself than any girl I've ever known!" I realized then what an incredible guy he was, and I fell in love with him on the spot.

Our relationship was tested early on by a girl at my highschool. She came to me and claimed that Marc slept around, and that he had slept with her, got her pregnant, pressured her to get an abortion, then dumped her. I told Marc about it, and he came to my school the next day to confront her. She was quite embarrassed because she had lied about the whole thing. She hoped I'd believe the lies and break up with Marc so she could have a shot at him. Later, Marc would admonish me, "Don't ever doubt my character." From that point on, I never did.

Marc and I, celebrating my first victory as the new Miss San Jose.

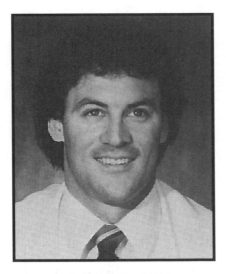

Marc Rebboah, "Prince Running Back". For 5 years, Marc trained me and inspired me to believe in myself.

My Stepmom Susie really helped me turn my life around. She encouraged me and held me accountable.

Chapter 14
Please Get Your Crown Out of My Refried Beans!

With Marc's help, I continued to train long and hard for the Miss California World pageant in June of 1980. I'd be competing against over 50 other girls for the crown.

When the day arrived, I was more than a bit nervous. While we were behind the scenes changing and doing make-up, the girls began to ask one another questions about their backgrounds. It became obvious to me that none of the other girls had a past quite like mine. The more I remembered the Sheri Rose I used to be, the more my anxiety level increased. I started feeling very unworthy of holding such an honorable title. Who wanted a Miss California World who was so insecure? Someone who had used drugs and alcohol, and who had come from a broken home? What kind of role model could I possibly be?

I was about ready to throw in the towel, when my dad walked up behind me and said, "Sheri, I'm so proud of you for what you've accomplished with your life." It's amazing what words of encouragement can do to a broken spirit. I was absolutely astonished that I finished the pageant as first runner-up! I was just as happy as if I had won!

I then realized that it was wrong for me to be ashamed of my past. It was my past that had helped mold my character. And, because I had conquered my past, I now had a story to tell that could encourage others. I decided that being a title-holder would be the perfect platform for sharing this story. So, I set my goal firmly on becoming Miss USA.

To make it to Miss USA, I'd have to change pageant systems. I'd first have to win a city pageant, and then a state pageant. Marc and I set our sights on Miss San Jose, coming up at the end of the year. I began to train harder than ever. I took public speaking courses, studied politics, read all the newspapers, signed up for modeling classes, enrolled in West Valley College, and even had my nose fixed.

The day of the Miss San Jose pageant arrived. I discovered the hard way that it takes practice to walk on a runway with a brightly focused spotlight shining directly in your face. When I came out for my walk, I could see absolutely nothing in front of me and I walked right off the end of the runway and landed flat on the judges' table! The audience gasped. Without missing a beat, I looked up at the judges with the perkiest smile I could muster and exclaimed, "I just wanted you to remember me!"

Evidently, they not only remembered me, they were impressed...and picked me to win! I was in shock! Later, one of the judges told me, "We thought that anyone who responded that well after something like *that*, deserved to win." Although this makes for a great story about how victory can come from what seems like tragedy—believe me, I don't recommend falling off the runway as a wise strategy for pageant contestants.

After the pageant, my clumsiness continued. We went to "pig out" at a Mexican restaurant for my reward. As I reached for a nacho, the crown toppled off my head and landed squarely in the refried beans and sour cream!

A few weeks later, I was driving to my very first appearance as Miss San Jose, when I discovered that my stepbrother Lanny had left the car on 'Empty'. I was running late and was already quite nervous. Now I was also angry. I stopped at a small family-owned gas station and the owner came out to serve me. He inserted the nozzle into my tank and turned on the pump. A few moments later, he came around to the driver's side to get the money. I was so flustered about being late, that I didn't realize my fill-up was still in progress. I thought that, since he was asking for the money, he must be finished already. I handed him the cash said, "thank you," and sped off!

Yes, that's right. I ripped the hose out of the pump while it was still pumping and drove away with the poor man's nozzle and hose hanging out of the side of my car! As I zoomed along to the location of my appearance, I noticed many people along the way waving at me and trying to get my attention. Since my picture had appeared in the paper, and I was wearing my regal crown, I concluded that these people must be my new adoring public, so I just smiled at them all and waved back!

When I arrived at the location, I was stunned to see the owner of the gas station pulling up behind me, panting and gasping. He'd been chasing me frantically through the streets of San Jose, and boy, was he upset. "You ruined my pump!" he screamed, hysterically. I was now more flustered than ever and didn't know quite what to say to the exasperated little fellow, so I offered him an autographed picture of me.

Refried beans and gas pump hoses notwithstanding, I was the new Miss San Jose. I was now eligible to compete for the state title, and I spent 1981 preparing for the Miss California pageant held in January of 1982 at Lake Tahoe. I was one of 110 girls who would be competing for the crown. The pageantry lasted an entire week, and the contestants' schedules were such that we were busy from 6:00 a.m. to midnight every day.

There were so many of us, that come mealtime, they had to shuttle us around in groups of 12 to various restaurants around the city. One night, my group was bused to a Chinese restaurant for dinner at about 9:00 p.m. At midnight, we still hadn't been picked up and began to realize that we'd been forgotten. It was freezing cold and snowing heavily. We called the hotel about our predicament, and prepared to wait it out, terribly depressed and angry about how dreadfully soon our 5:00 a.m. wake-up call was.

To make matters worse, the owners of the restaurant informed us that they had to close up and leave. We'd have to wait outside! We begged and pleaded for them not to kick us out into a blizzard. It was no use. We braved the elements until nearly 2:00 in the morning when we were finally picked up. The next morning (actually, four hours later!) all 12 of us were sick, but the promoters insisted we rise and shine to meet our schedules. They knew we couldn't refuse—not if we wanted a shot at winning.

Well, it didn't matter anyway, because I not only didn't win, I didn't even finish among the 12 semifinalists. I was depressed about it for months. If I still wanted to pursue my dream, I'd have to start over again by winning a city pageant. My heart wasn't in it, and I wanted to quit, but Marc and my dad both encouraged me to keep working. I next entered the 1982 Miss Bay Area pageant against 80 other girls and won. I was back on track for another run at a state pageant.

I worked hard but fell short again of the Miss California 1982 crown. After the state pageant, my mom got wind that I had competed (she was a former winner), and she called me from her new home in Idaho. I was thrilled to hear from her, since we'd barely spoken to one another since I'd moved out years earlier. She offered me encouragement and told me I was welcome to come and stay with her for awhile. I accepted.

During my visit, a recruiter for the Miss Idaho pageant saw me on the street and approached me about entering. Because of Idaho's smaller size, I wouldn't have to win a city pageant first. I was committed to competing for Miss California 1983, but Mom suggested that I should establish a dual residency and compete in both. So, for much of 1982, I traveled back and forth between California and Idaho, staying a few weeks at a time in each place.

Chapter 15

...Losers, Weepers

Not long after my loss at Miss California in '82, I was out at a modeling audition sitting in the waiting room with some of the other hopefuls. I looked around the room and was stunned to see several girls stuffing their faces with five or six candy bars each. Naturally, my curiosity got the best of me. "How can you eat like that and stay so thin?" I inquired.

"Oh, we just throw it up," came the reply. It shocked me all the more because it was said so casually, as if it were no big deal at all. We talked about it awhile, and I began to think I had discovered something wonderful. This is great, I thought. I'll never have to diet again. I could stay thin without having to work so hard for it, and I could eat all the treats I'd been denying myself for so long.

A few days later, after a big meal, I tried it. It grossed me out, but I liked knowing that all that food would never end up on my thighs. I started doing it every day, several times a day. I stopped dieting altogether. I also started taking laxatives, diuretics, and anything else I'd been told could give me a shortcut to my dream. I thought nothing of it's long term consequences and the devastating results on my health. No one knew what I was doing. The last thing I wanted was for Dad or Marc to find out that their precious Sheri Rose was now bulimic.

Marc's senior year at Santa Clara began amidst high expectations for the star running back. Things went well for him until one very tragic Saturday. While playing an away game in Reno, Nevada, Marc was "speared" in the back by an opposing player who rammed his helmet into Marc from behind.

He was rushed to the hospital. The doctors feared paralysis, and said he might never walk again. His father and I stood on opposite sides of his gurney, looking on with great concern. His father had always resented me. He took Marc's football very fanatically, and always forbade him to date during the season. Too much of a distraction, he felt, but Marc loved me so much that he refused to stop going out with me during the football seasons.

Seeing his boy in such a condition caused something to snap inside Marc's father, and he reached across the gurney and slapped me in the face. "It's all your fault!" he screamed. "He never would have let this happen if he wasn't dating you! I hope you're satisfied! Because whatever happens to him now is *your* responsibility!" Naturally, I freaked and ran out of the room crying hysterically.

Fortunately, Marc was ultimately able to walk out of the hospital. He'd be able to live a normal life, they said. With one major exception. They told him he'd *never* be able to play football again!

For awhile, Marc tried to compensate by putting all his energy into training me for Miss California and Miss Idaho, both in early 1983. I did much better for Miss California this time—second runner-up—but I was still depressed about not winning. We weren't licked yet, though. Miss Idaho was a only a few weeks away.

At the Idaho pageant, things went very smoothly. I was chosen as one of the finalists and was feeling very confident. Then came the 'question and answer' time. Questions were chosen at random and given to each of the finalists. When my turn came, the question I received was, "If you ever left Idaho, what would you miss the most?" Of all the questions, why did I get *that* one? I felt guilty about the dual residency. The only reason I was a resident at all in Idaho was for the pageant, and I knew in my heart that it would never be my home.

My mind raced. I had to come up with the perfect response, just as I had done the time I fell onto the judges table. But in the end, I couldn't bring myself to tell them what they wanted to hear—I decided to be completely honest. I told them that the question was a tough one, because I only lived in Idaho part-time. That probably cost me the victory—I was named first runner-up.

As hard as I took the losses, Marc took them especially hard. All the life seemed to drain out of him. He was left to face his own circumstances, and he became angry and bitter. He tried to overcome it as best he could, but there was no more fire in him. I seemed to have none to give him either, and our relationship began to spiral downward.

We made it through the next six stressful months, but we were clearly going nowhere. Marc sat me down for a talk. "I'll never be the Marc that I was," he began. "The person you loved...I'll never be that person again...and, I know you're not happy. So, I need to let you go!"

I could offer no argument. I choked back my tears long enough to say, "I love you, Marc. I'll *never* forget everything you've done for me." We both sobbed painfully and parted company for good. Our five year relationship had come to an end!

Chapter 16

I'll Be Happy When...

I began feeling lonely and insecure almost immediately after my break-up with Marc. After being with the same guy for so long, it felt foreign without a boyfriend. So, when a friend suggested we go dancing, I remembered the attention I got and the magic I experienced the night I saw Marc across the dance floor five years earlier. Maybe it could happen again.

As the evening progressed, I spotted a guy I thought was interesting. He was really cute, kind of quiet, and he wasn't drinking. So far, so good. I went over to strike up a conversation. "Hi, my name's Sheri, what's yours?"

"Kyman," he replied.

I laughed. "Are you married or something? Is that why you don't want to tell me your real name?"

He made a face. "Kyman *is* my real name."

"Well, Mr. Kyman, what's your *first* name?" I probed inquisitively.

"Kyman *is* my first name."

"Nice to meet you Kyman...Kyman what?" I pursued.

"Klimke. Kyman Klimke," He pronounced.

I'd like to say I bit my lip and kept my composure, but I didn't. I laughed right in his face and demanded to see his driver's license! At least *he* remained polite; offering proof of

67

his memorable name. After I removed my foot from my mouth, I managed to salvage the rest of the conversation, and we hit it off nicely. He asked for my phone number, and our dating relationship was off and running.

Unfortunately though, things weren't going quite so easily for my dad and his relationship with Susie. Their marriage was rocky and in trouble. They had moved to San Diego—a place Susie had always wanted to live—in a desperate attempt to save the marriage. Technically, I moved with them—certainly all my belongings were there—but most of the time I was on the road as part of my new career.

Early on in my experiences with pageantry, I had begun to see some real problems with the way most pageants were produced. At age 19, I discussed it with my father and told him I had a vision to produce pageants the way I believed they should be done. With his financial backing, and a great business manager named Connie Huggins, we started a production company and began to hold small pageants on the west coast.

It was difficult but rewarding work to produce a pageant and give a group of teenage girls an opportunity to realize their dreams. Rather than herd them around like cattle, I made sure they were treated with dignity and respect, and were allowed to have fun in the process.

The biggest and best pageant Connie and I produced was California's Golden Girl, held in July of 1983. It was televised live throughout the state of California—including Fox Television in Los Angeles.

After conquering my goal as pageant producer, I was ready to move on to something different. My dad, being from Hollywood, said there were vast numbers of people who wanted to become actors and models, but did not have the contacts to get started. He recommended that, instead of producing pageants, I start producing modeling and acting showcases and partner with Top-40 radio stations to promote the events. These showcases would give aspiring models and actors a tremendous opportunity to show their talent to agencies, casting directors, and producers. My cousin, Barry, was a respected personal manager in Hollywood and he provided me with some great industry contacts.

In 1984, we tested the marketplace for these showcases in San Jose, California, and it was an overwhelming success— and the birth of a new career for me. So off we went, to San Diego, for the next one. Although I enjoyed directing these showcases, and was thankful that they were so successful, deep inside, I felt as lost and empty as when I was a child. Sometimes, I felt like I was just going through the motions, and I started losing my passion for life. Ironically, it was during this time that I was named one of America's Most Outstanding Young Women for everything I'd achieved. It amazed me that people saw me as "outstanding" when internally I was falling apart.

During the San Diego showcase, I was particularly drawn to a very talented singer named Joyce Wells. Although she had a tremendous gift for belting out a song, she remained humble and unaffected by the praises everyone gave her. She was kind and sensitive, with a terrific sense of humor. I couldn't help but want to get to know her more, so I invited her to go to San Francisco with me to help with the next showcase. She agreed, and became my new business partner—and quickly became my new best friend as well.

Well, now I really 'had it all'. A steady boyfriend, a best friend to travel with, a thriving business. What more could a girl want? But something was obviously still missing, because I was as depressed as ever. I was a victim of the 'I'll be happy when' syndrome. Maybe I'll be happy when I get a boyfriend— no, that didn't do it. Maybe I'll be happy when I'm thinner, or tanner, or when my hair is longer—no, those things didn't do it either. Maybe I'll be happy when I find the perfect dress, or when I find the right friend, or when I make a certain amount of money. But none of these things filled the horribly empty void I felt in my heart.

Of course, I was still bulimic, and it was ruining my health. Ironically, in spite of my bulimia, I had still managed somehow to gain back 20 pounds. Through it all, my family situation was still a mess. I once again had no relationship with my mom, and my dad's marriage was crumbling rapidly, making it hard to turn to Dad or Susie for anything.

Keeping busy working 12 hours a day, surrounding myself with people, having Joyce travel with me— these were the ways I tried to avoid being alone to face the truth. But at the end of each day, I'd have no choice but to reflect on my life and succumb to an intensely dark cloud of depression. One night it was so bad that I felt like I was reaching my breaking point. I fell to my knees and cried out, "God, please help me!" Little did I realize at that moment just what He had in store for me.

The following day, as I talked to Kyman about the San Francisco Showcase and how depressing it is to live out of hotel rooms, he told me that Joyce and I were welcome to stay with his grandparents. They were Christian missionaries who lived in a six bedroom house they had owned for forty years, and were quite accustomed to having house guests. They often provided a place to stay for missionaries passing through the area. I had met his grandparents once before and really enjoyed their company. I discussed it with Joyce, and we decided to take them up on their offer.

Joyce and I arrived in San Francisco just in time to experience some of the worst weather the Bay area had ever seen for the month of April. It was freezing cold, raining intensely, and unbearably windy, even by San Francisco's standards.

On the second morning of the event, we set out for the showcase site armed with a stack of applications from actors and models who had made it through the previous day's auditions. As we stepped out of the car in the pouring rain, Joyce's foot slipped on the glassy slick pavement and sent her into majestic, showgirl-style splits. In one dramatic motion, her skirt ripped all the way up her backside as the wind tore the stack of papers from her hand! She went flying one way while the rain soaked papers blew another. There was no time to laugh or cry. We immediately kicked into "Desperation Mode"! We were parked on one of the city's notoriously steep hills at the time, and the applications were now sailing downhill at a rapid clip, bouncing and twirling in the rain gutter.

We had no choice but to run after them. Joyce's dignity was more at stake than mine, since her backside was now exposed to the elements and the rest of the world.

"Help! Help! Please stop those papers!" we screamed frantically to people on the street below. A few did lend a hand, but most decided we surely were mentally unbalanced and gave us a wide berth as we ran pell-mell down the hill, arms flailing wildly.

I doubt whether we instilled a lot of confidence in the crew that day when we walked in with hair and clothes completely soaked, make-up hopelessly smeared, carrying our stack of dripping applications. We did as many call-backs from the auditions as we could, but water had rendered some of the applications illegible, and the wind had carried a few away into the San Francisco Bay. Joyce and I later joked about the possibility that some future superstar might never be discovered because of our mishap.

In the evenings, as I got to know Kyman's grandparents, Charlie and Emily, they told me stories about some of their experiences as missionaries in Rumania where they had worked to give food and Bibles to hopeless, poverty stricken people behind the Iron Curtain. In those days, amid the evils of a communist regime, it was impossible for Christian missionaries to go into Rumania without putting their lives in danger. In many cases, missionaries were put to death for sharing the Word of God. It amazed me that these two loving 70 year old people would risk their lives to meet the needs of others. It was obvious that there was something very special about these two wonderful people, and I was intrigued to know more.

Charlie and Emily had been married for over 40 years and were still very much in love. I noticed that they read the Bible every morning and prayed together. They actually sat at the table and had meals together like a real family and—I couldn't help noticing—they loved me and accepted me uncon-ditionally. I didn't have to accomplish anything great to obtain their approval. Whatever they had that made them the way they were, I wanted it! But when they tried to share their faith with me, I was defensive. Each Sunday when they invited me to attend church with them, I declined. For one thing, I'd been raised Jewish. I thought I'd be turning against my father, who had always expressed a strong anti-Christian bias.

Joyce remained faithfully by my side each Sunday. Little did I realize at the time how much she wanted to join them at church. Joyce, as it turns out, was a Christian too. But when she saw how defensive I became when Charlie and Emily attempted to talk to me about Jesus, she decided that God had more work to do on my hard heart, and, as was her way, she quietly committed the matter to prayer.

Charlie and Emily decided not to pressure me anymore on my last Sunday at their house, so they didn't invite me to go to church with them. Instead, they prayed that God would incline my heart to want to go. Well, it worked. I actually asked them if it would be alright if I went with them. At the church service, several people were brought to the front to tell how Jesus had taken their broken lives and put them back together again. They shared how they came to put God first in their lives, and how He had given them purpose and direction. It certainly seemed that God was trying to tell me something!

Joyce and I finally had to say good-bye to our new missionary friends and prepared for our next showcase in Fresno in late spring of 1984. We hoped to avoid anything resembling a repeat of our adventure in San Francisco's weather, but much to our despair, it was rainy and quite foggy when we arrived.

The radio station that we were partnered with on the showcase had loaned us their van to use while in town. We should have realized we were in for another one of those days when we ran over the bellman's toe at the hotel! He tried hard to 'be tough' and pretend it was no big deal, but we could see the poor man was in terrible pain.

It was so foggy by the time we reached the freeway that we had to open the van doors to see the lines on the road.

Finally, we were too frightened to go any further and pulled over to wait out the weather. Hours later, the people at the radio station became concerned about our absence and called the police to search for us. Just another day in the life of Sheri Rose and company.

After Fresno, I returned to San Jose to see Kyman. I wanted Joyce to come with me, but she couldn't. That meant I'd be staying in the hotel alone each night. I wasn't looking forward to that. As long as I was busy, or with someone, I didn't have to think about my life. I dreaded being alone more than just about anything, but this time, I'd discover that I had never really been alone after all.

Chapter 17

Free Indeed!

So there I was in my hotel room in San Jose, California on a hot summer night in 1984. I was scared, lonely, and very depressed. I had tried on my own to straighten out my life as best I could, but nothing was working. I tried desperately to stop the bulimia, but the harder I tried to quit, the worse it became. I felt that I'd never be able to escape the clutches of this horrible sickness.

My kidneys were failing, my teeth were rotting, I had terrible headaches, I couldn't sleep at night, I had a hernia the size of a baseball from all the vomiting, and I had pains in my heart almost all the time. And after all this torture, I was still overweight!

"I can't live like this anymore, I thought. I can't go on pretending to be some kind of "outstanding young woman". I had set my standards so high, that they were impossible to live up to. I tried to comfort myself at night by ordering six desserts from room service. I ate them all, then immediately threw them up and started to cry. My head was pounding, my stomach ached, my heart hurt, and I began hyper-ventilating.. At that moment I noticed the bottle of sleeping pills by the side of my bed. I decided I'd had enough. I wanted to end it all.

In a final act of desperation, I fell to my knees and cried out, "Jesus, if you're there, please stop me from killing myself!

They tell me you are "the Way". If that's true, then come into my heart and fix my broken life."

I'll never forget the moment I prayed that prayer, because God gave me the peace that I had been so desperately searching for. It was as if God Himself had reached down and wrapped his arms around me! I fell into the deepest, most peaceful sleep I'd ever experienced. Then I started to dream, and in my dreams I saw clearly how many times in my life God had tried to get my attention.

I remembered junior high and how Keith's Christian parents had loved me. I remembered my highschool friend who had been dealing drugs, but came back from a church camp totally transformed. Instead of dealing drugs, he started leading Bible studies for the lonely, unpopular kids at our school.

I remembered a time about four years earlier when I ran out of gas, and a nice young man stopped to help me. Since I had no money, he used his own money to get me gas and fill my tank. When I asked how I could pay him back, he handed me a pamphlet about Jesus, and said, "Just read this if you want to pay me back." Mostly though, I remembered my missionary friends, Emily and Charlie, because that same peace that had surrounded me during my stay in their home *was now inside me!* Maybe it was the prayers of all these wonderful people that brought me to this very point. When I awoke the next morning from this peaceful slumber, my five-year battle with bulimia had ended in victory!

Later that day, I went to work out at a nearby health club. In the middle of my work-out, two girls came up to me and asked me, "Are you a Christian?" I couldn't believe this was happening.

"It's funny you should ask," I smiled. I told them about

my experience the previous evening. One of the girls introduced herself as Anna and invited me to lunch.

Over lunch, we shared our stories. As we were finishing,
she invited me to check out of the hotel and come to stay with
her and her husband Scott, who worked in ministry. God sure
moves fast sometimes, I thought, and I accepted her offer.

Over the next few months, as I lived with Anna and
Scott, I continued to grow in my faith and develop my
relationship with the Lord. I was so excited about what God
had done for me—and *in* me—that I wanted to tell the world.
I began sharing the Gospel with friends, grocery store clerks,
gas station attendants, health club employees, and anyone else
who would listen. But as much as I wanted to share these
things with my Jewish family, I was just too afraid of their
reaction. Right before Thanksgiving, I flew home to San Diego
to be with Dad and Susie for the holidays. I admit that I had
it in the back of my mind that I might be able to 'fix' their
troubled relationship with my newfound faith.

Susie could tell right away that there was something
dramatically different about me. When we were alone, she
pressed me for the details. I thought I'd burst if I didn't share
it with her, so I told her that I had accepted the Lord. I couldn't
believe my ears when she said, "So did I!"

"What?? What do you mean? When?"

"I was watching a Christian television broadcast and
they shared about God's love and forgiveness," she replied. "I
realized that I needed to put God first in my life." She also
admitted that she, too, was afraid to tell Dad about it. So,
whenever Dad was gone, Susie and I would watch Christian
television and listen to contemporary Christian music by
artists like Carman, Michael W. Smith, Sandi Patti, and Amy

Grant. And, of course, we prayed for my dad. I also had Anna, Scott, and my friend Joyce praying for him, too.

I was determined that things would be different in my family relationships from this point on. For one thing, I made a commitment that, while I was at home, I would not let Dad buy anything for me. Normally, I would have welcomed his lavish gestures, but I knew now that money was not the answer to life's problems.

Dad did insist that I at least let him take me out to dinner one night. I agreed, and during the dinner, Dad said, "Sheri, you are *so* different. You've never looked more beautiful, and you've never seemed so peaceful...so strong. I can't remember when I've enjoyed your company more. You haven't been whiny and you haven't been crying or acting irritated like you used to. You're like a breath of fresh air." Here was an opening if I'd ever heard one.

"Well...," I began slowly, "yes, I am different." I proceeded to tell him that no matter how well things seemed to be going before, I just wasn't happy. I told him about the bulimia and about the night I decided to commit suicide.

I stopped for a moment, because I noticed his eyes were welling up with tears. "Why would you want kill yourself?" he pleaded.

I explained that I felt as though my life had no purpose and that I had no reason to go on. "The only reason I'm alive right now is because I don't have to carry my burdens alone anymore...." I then told him what had happened and how I had given my life to God. I had been afraid he'd explode if I mentioned the name Jesus, but his reaction took me completely by surprise. He continued to listen in a way that was more gentle and more attentive than I can ever remember in my life.

"I'm just so thankful that you're okay now," he said, "and I'm so sorry that I didn't know you were going through all of this." He raised his eyebrow and smiled but he warned me not to say anything about it to the rest of our Jewish family, especially Grandma Sadie.

When we got home that night, I gave Susie a look that told her something was up, but Dad was standing right there, so I had to try and get her alone. "Uhhh...I think I'm gonna go to bed now. Susie, would you...uh...come and tuck me in?"

"Tuck you in??" Dad raised his eyebrows, "For heaven's sake, Sheri, you're 24 years-old!" Hey, I know, but it was the only thing I could think of at the time. I waited until the next day to tell Susie. She was thrilled that he took it so well, and we began to pray for Dad harder than ever. Eventually, Susie would also come to tell Dad about the Lord, partly in an attempt to save their failing marriage.

A month or so later, I was in Los Angeles to audition for a job as a TV talk-show host. Joyce was once again by my side. One good look at L.A., though, and I realized I didn't want to live there. I wondered if I should even go through with the audition, knowing that I really didn't want the job after all. I decided to call and talk to Dad about it. It was during that conversation that he told me about my grandmother. "She's dying, Sheri. She only has a few weeks left."

"Where is she?" I asked. He said she was at home, being cared for by a 24-hour nurse he had provided for her. "I have to go and see her while I'm here," I told him.

"That'd be great, Sheri, but please remember not to tell her about the Jesus thing, okay?"

In my heart I knew that God wanted His children to share His message of love, and I was torn as to what to do.

I confided in Joyce. "My grandma's had such an unhappy life," I told her. "Except for my dad, all her children abandoned her. Then my grandpa died, and she's been so alone." Joyce comforted me and encouraged me that I should go ahead and tell Grandma about the peace I had found in Jesus.

I remember the huge knot I felt in my stomach as I entered Grandma's house. I looked around to see photos of me and records of my accomplishments everywhere I turned. She loved me so dearly. I knew how much she bragged about me to her friends during their card-playing sessions. I took a deep breath and went to kneel at her bedside. I gently laid my body over hers, and told her, "Grandma, please don't die." Then I began to share about Jesus with her. Immediately, she turned her back on me and demanded that I leave her house.

"*You* are the one who's dead. You are no longer my granddaughter." Her words completely crushed me. I loved her so very much, and had hoped to share with her a precious and eternal gift, but now she wanted nothing to do with me. Of course, Dad found out and was furious. After screaming at me, he, too, refused to speak to me, and I was specifically asked *not* to attend her funeral when she passed away several weeks later.

I had a tough time accepting that this could happen. Why would God allow things to turn out so badly? Ultimately, I know that God sees *beyond* the here and now. He promised that His plans are for Blessing, but sometimes we miss It because we cling *too* tightly—and to the *wrong* things. Yes, He *is* a God of judgement, but He is equally a God of mercy. Somewhere between the two, we often entangle ourselves and must cling to Faith to bring us to salvation, peace and victory.

My best friend, Joyce, and I have been through everything together. A great singer, business partner, and counselor.

Joyce and I choreographed dance production numbers and hosted the show-cases together.

Kyman was always a big help when I produced events in the Bay Area. He also introduced me to his missionary grandparents.

I learned some great things from my spiritual "mom", Emily. She and her husband, Charlie, of 40 years, are the most generous and caring people I have ever know.

Chapter 18

God and Tuna

After my visit with Dad and Susie, I went back to San Jose to stay with Anna and Scott, and I continued to pray for God to direct my steps. Shortly thereafter, the director of the upcoming Miss Idaho Pageant, Marta Cheatham, called to invite me to compete. "This is the last year you'll be eligible to go for Miss USA," she reminded me. "Next year, you'll be too old." I told her that winning a pageant wasn't very important to me anymore, and I explained that I was now a Christian.

"Well, as a matter of fact, Sheri, I'm a Christian too," she revealed, "and I think this would be an ideal platform for you to share what God's done in your life."

"As a beauty queen?" I expressed my doubt. "How could a beauty queen ever tell about Jesus? I mean, it's so...worldly."

"Sheri, whatever you have, you give it to God. Lay it at the Cross, and He'll use it. Period," she replied. "It doesn't matter if you're an actor, a model, a construction worker or whatever." I realized Marta was right and decided to go for it.

I called my mom in Idaho and told her about my new faith, and about my decision to compete again. I then asked if I could stay with her again, as I did the last time I went for Miss Idaho. She was reluctant at first. For one thing, I think she was a little numb to me emotionally. She felt that I'd hurt her on so many occasions. And I'm sure she considered the fact that I was only coming to be with her so I could be in the pageant. In the end, she said yes.

It wasn't easy going, though. True, we were under the same roof again, but Mom seemed more distant than ever. For most of my stay in Idaho, I felt out-of-place and quite lonely.

When pageant time came, my new faith caused a dramatic change in my attitude. I wasn't the least bit obsessed about how I looked or what I wore. I did a very simple make-up job, and wore a rather plain dress. It was burgundy, of all colors—rather unheard of in pageant circles (I even wore a pair of high-top tennis shoes to the reception!). Instead of paying fanatical attention to how I looked, I spent the three hours before the start of the pageant in prayer. I simply told the Lord, "God, this is yours. Whatever You want to happen is fine with me." A few hours later, I was the new Miss Idaho!

In response to questions by the press, I gave the glory and credit for my victory to God, and also told them that my current diet consisted largely of tuna fish, eggs, and brown rice. The next day, one of the headlines read, "MISS IDAHO THANKS GOD AND TUNA."

It was on to Florida in the spring of '85 for the pageant I used to dream of winning—Miss USA. But now, as with Miss Idaho, I held no obsession for this crown—what I wanted most was to be the best ambassador for the Lord that I could. I shared the Gospel with many of the girls, some of whom decided during our time together that they, too, wanted to put their faith and trust in the Lord. I was thrilled. God also had blessed me with a Christian buddy, Debra Strauss, Miss Wisconsin.

Our lack of obsession with winning allowed us to thoroughly enjoy the entire experience. 'i'll never forget the fun I had and the friends I made. When it was over, I didn't even make it into the top 10 semi-finalists, but it didn't bother me in the least. I can't tell you how terrific I felt when some of the girls came to me afterward and said, "Sheri, you kept telling us all along that winning wasn't the most important thing to you, and you just wanted to please God. So we were watching you when you lost to see how you'd react. Sheri, you're really genuine. Your faith is truly real."

New Miss Idaho thanks God, tuna

BOISE (UPI) The new Miss Idaho-U.S.A. said Sunday she has God and canned tuna to thank for her victory in the pageant.

Sheri Rose of Hammett, who won the title Saturday after competing for three years in a row, said becoming a Christian last year made the big difference this time around.

"I really think my success is owed to that. I really do. I feel that when I became a Christian it gave me the inner beauty I needed," she said.

The slender 23-year-old also gives quick — if less serious — credit to the canned tuna she lived on during the four days of last week's pageant.

"When I first got the schedule for the contest and saw all the restaurants where we were supposed to eat, I knew I had to do something," she said.

So, when she arrived in Boise for the competition, she brought six cans of tuna with her. "That's all I ate, tuna with mustard, and tofu and crackers," she said. "If I ever see tuna again I'll shoot it."

Rose said she has been fighting a weight problem since age 16 when she was more than 40 pounds overweight. She now stands 5-foot-7-inches and weighs 115 pounds.

Other winners in the contest were Chris Dahlberg, Nampa, first runner-up; Deana Gustaves, Boise, second runner-up; Stacy Beardon, Idaho Falls, third runner-up; and Michelle Ruby, Moscow, fourth runner-up.

Born in Los Angeles, Rose came from California to Idaho four years ago to live with an aunt in Hammett. She runs her own business in Boise where she conducts seminars to motivate teen-age girls who want careers in entertainment and modeling.

Among the spoils of her victory will be a scholarship to a Boise modeling school, a cash award based on pageant re-

ceipts, a wardrobe and a trip to Florida to compete in the Miss U.S.A. contest in Florida in May.

The director of the state pageant, a former Miss Idaho-U.S.A herself, said she thinks Rose's chances in the national contest are excellent. "I really feel she's going to do something good for Idaho this year," said Marta Cheatle.

Rose said she plans to move to Boise in a couple of weeks so she and Cheatle can work closely on lining up public appearances to prepare her for the competition with women from all 50 states.

"Most people don't realize how much preparation goes into a national pageant that lasts two-and-a-half weeks," Cheatle said. "She'll need all the poise and confidence she can muster."

A total of 19 Idaho women competed in the pageant, held Wednesday through Saturday at Boise State University. About 600 persons attended the final night of competition at BSU's Morrison Center for the Performing Arts.

In Daybreak
Sheri Rose of Hammett to compete Monday for Miss USA 1985 crown
— Page 1D

Quite an interesting headline, don't you think?
At least I have my priorities straight!

My first State Crown, Miss Idaho USA, 1985. I was finally on my way to Miss USA after 5 years of trying!

Chapter 19

The Dating Game

Toward the end of the month-long Miss USA event, I had my 25th birthday, May 8, 1985. Early that day, while walking through the pageant site at the Lakeland Convention Center in Florida, I had spotted posters announcing that the contemporary Christian music artist, Carman, would be in concert that night in one of the Center's many auditoriums. Also scheduled for that evening in a different part of the center, was a dance for all of the girls in the pageant. How great it would be to perhaps meet Carman that night, I thought. I listened to his music all the time. My stepmom, Susie, had introduced me to his music, and went so far as to say to me, "Sheri, I think you should meet Carman some day and marry him."

Little did I know that morning, that while I was reading the concert posters, Carman was having a conversation with Miss Florida, who informed him that there was a Christian in the pageant—Sheri Rose, Miss Idaho! At lunch time, Carman's manager came to find me and bring me best wishes from Carman. I gave her a note to take back to Carman, in which I wrote, "I love your music, and I respect you for what you're doing. You're a great witness for Jesus!" She then snapped a picture of me and took it to him along with the note.

That night while I was at the dance, I suddenly heard my name being paged. As soon as I heard my name, I somehow knew that it was Carman looking for me—he had walked over to the dance after he'd finished his concert. We then went to talk, accompanied by my "chaperone"—one of the female security guards assigned to the girls to protect us when in public (It turns out that even the security guard was a Christian!).

We had a great time getting to know one another—we talked about his music, about my production company, and about the pageant. "So do you think you'll win?" he asked. I told him it was up to God. He smiled and said that he'd like to see me again. I agreed.

After a few weeks passed, he had his mom call my mom on the phone. "How adorably clever and old-fashioned," I thought. They ended up talking on the phone many times—about us, of course—and even wrote to each other, swapping snapshots (including baby pictures!) as well as stories. Then his family invited me to come to their home in Anaheim, California, for a four-day visit, and I accepted. It was understood that Carman wouldn't be there— he was still on the road—but he'd call every night so we could talk. The most amazing thing about my visit was that his mother and father's personality were exactly like my grandma and grandpa's. It was uncanny! I felt as though God had, in His own way, given my grandparents back to me for a few precious days.

God had also restored my relationship with my dad during this time, so in June, I went back to San Diego to stay with Dad and Susie. Susie almost fell over when I told her about meeting Carman. She was even more excited about it than I was. I told her I had left it in God's hands, and that He would guide me in the matter.

Meanwhile, I continued to produce showcases. Joyce and I headed for Phoenix, Arizona for our next event, accompanied this time by my Miss USA Pageant roommate, Debra Strauss, Miss Wisconsin. The local photographer we hired for the event brought an assistant with him—a charming twenty year-old college student and model named Michael. We were immediately attracted to each other, but he was five years younger than I was, and I wanted to be wise and keep a safe distance. Every time I turned around, it seemed, there was Michael offering to help me or paying me some compliment. He then asked if I wanted to go out dancing with some friends that night. I declined the offer, but agreed to meet him for breakfast the net morning in the hotel restaurant.

When I arrived at breakfast, I found that Michael had decorated the booth ahead of time with streamers, balloons, cards, glitter, you name it. On one of the cards he had written, "You're the most beautiful woman in the world." This is adorable but completely crazy, I thought.

"So can we go out dancing *tonight*?" he persisted as we finished our breakfast. I was still pretty reluctant and unsure about it all.

"He's only 20," I reminded myself, but as we exited the restaurant, I looked up to see that, during the middle of the night, he somehow managed to scale a nearby billboard to hang a sign that read, "Sheri, will you go out with me?" Did this guy read from the same book as my dad or what? I just couldn't say no after all this.

Meanwhile, every day of the showcase, Michael would make gestures like sending me flowers, balloons, poetry, and cards, some of which had pictures of the two of us pasted inside, and he remained a gentleman through it all. After I flew home to San Diego, I had more of an opportunity to think clearly about the potential problems in having some kind of relationship with Michael. Two problems in particular stood out—the obvious age difference and the fact that we lived in different states. I missed him alot, but I couldn't help thinking it was unrealistic to pursue a relationship.

Ultimately, my heart won out over my head, and I decided to continue seeing Michael. I looked forward to flying to Phoenix a few times a month because Michael was always full of surprises and I enjoyed being with him. I was also still seeing Kyman whenever I was in San Jose. Neither knew specifically about the other, but I did tell each of them that our relationship wasn't exclusive. That had never stopped Kyman from talking about marriage, and now, it wasn't keeping Michael from talking about it either. My responses always managed to resemble some form of 'maybe', which didn't exactly discourage them.

Now let me backtrack a bit to tell you about Peter. During the Phoenix showcase where I'd met Michael, Joyce and I would go to a health club to work out and attend aerobics classes. It was at one of these classes that I met Peter. He gave a note to one of the club employees to bring over to me. The note read, "I enjoyed watching you doing aerobics. Will you have lunch with me?" The employee pointed in the direction of the handsome 32 year-old who wrote the note. I wrote 'Yes' on the note and gave it back to the employee to take to Peter.

I turned to Joyce and asked, "You don't mind, do you?"

"Oh, of course not. What's one more guy? We'll just add him to the end of the string," she teased.

She then walked over to Peter with tongue-in-cheek and told him, "If you're smart you won't fall for her. Her nickname is The Destroyer".

This didn't phase him a bit, and off we went to lunch. It didn't take me long to work Jesus into the conversation, and Peter began to challenge my faith by asking me the usual tough questions that skeptics have. When lunch was over, he said he wanted to see more of me, and I felt like I wanted to keep sharing about

God with him, so I said yes. After I returned to San Diego, Peter would fly there occasionally to see me, and I'd pick him up at the airport or meet him somewhere. I didn't want guys coming to the house, since Dad was still as possessive as ever.

After I'd been back in San Diego for a few months, I developed some neck pain and asked Joyce to take me to my chiropractor for an adjustment. My regular doctor was gone that day for some reason, and in his place was an adorable 30 year-old chiropractor named David.

"Is he gorgeous or what?" I whispered to Joyce. "How am I supposed to relax so he can adjust me?"

Joyce rolled her eyes. "Oh no, here we go again. Well, let's see, when can we squeeze him in?" She picked up a magazine and pretended it was an appointment book. "Hmmm. Well you might be able to squeeze him in on Wednesday between 11:30 and 11:45. Then you'll have to catch a plane to spend 45 minutes with Michael in Phoenix, then—."

"Okay, okay! I get your point!" I chuckled.

"But it's not going to stop you, is it?' she eyed me suspiciously.

"Well... No." We both roared with laughter.

"Fine," she gave in. "So how are you going to get him to ask you out?"

"Well, I'll let him do an adjustment now, then I'll call the emergency number tonight and say my neck's out again." And that's exactly what I did. He came over that night, adjusted my neck again, and we began to talk. In fact, we stayed up until one a.m. talking about God and a hundred other topics. Before he left, he asked me out for the next day.

Ironically, while I was talking to David, my stepmom Susie was fielding my phone calls and took messages from Carman,

Kyman, Michael, and Peter! Good heavens, what was I doing?? It's not that I was trying to play games or be some kind of play-girl. I really wanted to be in a monogamous relationship and get married, but I was afraid of marrying the wrong person, so every time I met a new guy who seemed nice, I'd think, hey, maybe *he's* supposed to be the one. In my mixed-up mind, I thought the "guy" picture would just somehow clear itself up. But each of these guys had different qualities that I loved and admired, so instead of the picture getting clearer, it only became muddier.

Michael in Phoenix continued to be an incredibly persistent guy. He asked me over and over again if he could come to San Diego to meet my family, and each time he asked, I told him no. He was probably the *last* guy I'd want to meet my father! Even without meeting Michael, Dad was already suspicious. He noticed that I dressed differently when I was on my way to see Michael than I did at other times. All the other guys were in their late-20s or early-30s, but Michael was a 20 year-old college kid. We usually hung out in "college" places with a college crowd, so I would dress the way college kids dressed in 1985. Remember? It was fun for me, because I'd never had the "college experience" and now I was getting a taste of what I'd missed, but Dad wasn't sure he wanted his little girl dressing like Madonna, so it was a sore subject.

Let me point something out to you before I continue. It was-n't until after I met my husband that I understood just how naive I was about men, and temptation and lust. I had no idea back then that, even though my motives were pure, my style of dress and friendly attitude was causing men to misunderstand me.

Well, Michael's mind was made up to continue pursuing me. He hopped on a plane one day and came to San Diego without any warning. He just showed up at our front door! Dad hated him instantly—no surprise there—but I noticed that, with Michael,

Dad was even snottier than usual, so I was suspicious when Dad later offered to take us out to dinner.

During dinner Dad was as cold and sarcastic to Michael as he could be. Then from out of nowhere, my father, who never had trouble saying what was on his mind, leaned forward, pointed a finger at Michael and said, "Boy, if you ever, EVER, lay a hand on my daughter, I'll break your neck." I was mortified. I lashed out at Dad for behaving this way, and the battle was on. Dad told Michael to leave and go back to Phoenix. I thought this might actually be the wisest course of action at this point, and said so to Michael.

Then Michael, who perhaps was more like my dad than I wanted to admit, stiffened his neck in total defiance. "You can't tell me what to do!" he snarled. "Sheri's an adult and she can make her own decisions. If she wants to see me, then we'll see each other!" Dad went positively berserk. He wasn't used to someone standing up to him like this, especially some snot-nosed punk with designs on his baby girl.

Back at home, Dad not only hadn't calmed down, but seemed to be growing angrier. He screamed and yelled at me for hours, until I finally snapped and stormed up to my room and began to pack. "Where do you think you're going?" he bellowed.

"I'm moving out. I'm going to Phoenix to be with Michael." That was the last thing he wanted to hear, but it did slow him down a bit, since it made him realize he was all but pushing me out the door. His attempts to change my mind fell on deaf ears, however. I was going, and that was that. But I will never forget what Dad said to me as I was on my way out the door, "Just so you know, Sheri. This guy will never let you go. If you ever try to break up with him, he'll try to kill you."

I drove to Phoenix with those words still ringing in my

ears. As I began a new year (1986) and a new life in the "Valley of the Sun", I slowly began to see Michael in a somewhat different light. Being in such close proximity now, he was around all the time, and I mean *all the time*. His constant attention toward me started to wear on me, and as I began to exhibit signs of frustration over it, he grew more possessive and more controlling with each passing day. I started to panic a bit. Perhaps my father was right. I wished that I could talk to Dad about it, but once again, he wasn't speaking to me.

I soon discovered another cause for concern—I was running out of money. It was time to do another showcase, I thought. I called Joyce and asked her to come to Arizona to help. But without Dad's reputation and influence with the media, we were unable to persuade a radio station to partner with us. We'd have to pay for the air-time to promote the event. That meant we had to come up with about $10,000.

Michael decided this would be the perfect opportunity to join the business with me, and he managed to convince a friend of his to loan us the money, but Michael's attitude during the showcase proved to be as controlling as it was in our relationship. He seemed to want to run the whole show, and it irritated me beyond measure. That, I resolved, was the last straw.

Toward the end of the event, I took Michael aside and told him, "Look. This just isn't going to work. I don't want to be with you anymore. I want you out of my life and out of my company. We're through."

"Oh no we're not. You're can't leave me," came his chilling response. I could once again hear my father's words of warning to me when I left San Diego. A huge fight ensued between us, and I was so frightened that I felt I needed to get as far away from him as possible for awhile. I'd been living in the same apartment complex as Michael, but with the help of Atwood, a new friend, I was able to sneak my stuff out without Michael's knowledge, and Joyce and I moved into an apartment in Mesa, just outside of Phoenix.

I was feeling pretty burned out from the "guy" situation, and decided to take a break from men for awhile. I kept busy and distracted by absorbing myself in producing showcases. There was one particular man I really wanted to hear from—my dad—but he wasn't speaking to me. It would take a miracle to fix things between us. So I prayed to God for one. And a miracle is just what He gave me.

When the phone rang in my apartment that day in 1986, I was surprised to hear my dad's voice on the other end of the line. I knew that Dad and Susie had been struggling and I thought that he's probably calling because he's sad and lonely, but I couldn't have been more wrong. What he said next made my head spin.

"I have a lot to thank Susie for," he began. For one thing, your brother (Michael) is now a Christian." I barely had time to catch my breath from this incredible news when he added, "First I saw what Jesus did for you, and now I've seen what He's done for Michael, and, well, I started to think maybe He's real after all. Then the other day, I was watching a program on Christian television, and it made me realize that I need a relationship with Jesus Christ too."

I sobbed great tears of joy and happiness. My father had been a proud, strong, and controlling man, and now here he was, telling me, "I've always tried to do things *my* way. Now I realize that a *real* man is one who does things *God's* way." My father, who had been as anti-Christian as anyone I'd ever known, now embraced Jesus as the Messiah, the Savior. Yes, the Lord really does answer prayer, and miracles really do happen.

My modeling composite when I lived in
Phoenix in 1985.

The 1985 Miss
USA opening
production
number, featur-
ing "Cool and
the Gang", held
in Lakeland,
Florida.

Chapter 20

A Few Good Men

While I was attempting to keep my distance from men for awhile, Carman called to say he was coming to Phoenix to do a concert and wanted to see me while he was in town. We spent some nice time together, but I began to get the feeling that it just wasn't "meant to be" between us. His life was so incredibly hectic, I just didn't see how I'd fit into it. When he left, I tried once again to keep "finding Mr. Right" from becoming such a high priority in my life. I tried leaving it in God's hands, but as 1986 wore on, I began to feel lonely again.

While the other guys were more mature, more sophisticated, and more stable, Michael was the most fun and the most romantic, and I really missed that. I decided to call him and reconcile. We began to date again, but not before I made it as clear as possible that I intended to see other people as well. This however, didn't deter him from pursuing me with his usual vigor. One night, as we were sitting together in church, he pulled out a ring and asked me to marry him! "Maybe this is a sign that he's the one," I thought. After all, we *were* in *church*, and Michael always made me feel so special.

In retrospect, I realize the decision was based purely on emotion—not in the least on faith and logic—but I said yes. He promptly announced it to everyone in the church that night, but telling a crowd of church-goers was easy compared to the job that awaited me—telling my dad.

I went home to San Diego to break the news to Dad. Dad didn't hit the ceiling when I told him (he knew better), he just told me we were both in "La-La Land" and that it would never last. I was stubborn and wouldn't budge on the issue. "Remember when you and Mom were going to get married, how people tried to talk you out of it? You didn't listen—you did what you thought was right," I argued.

"Yeah, and look how that turned out," he countered, "that's why I know it won't work for you, Sheri—it's history repeating itself! Please don't make the same mistake I did with your mom!" Dad was deeply grieved that his point fell on deaf ears. Gradually, he came to accept it, but just as my father started getting used to the idea, I started having second thoughts. I had made the big decision! I had committed to this one man and fixed all my hopes on the idea that he, and not one of the others, was the man I should spend the rest of my life with. I started becoming anxious and afraid.

In the middle of this confusion, David (the chiropractor) called and suggested we go out to dinner. At the restaurant, I tried to find an appropriate moment to tell him I was now engaged to another man, but David wasn't making it easy for me. He was the most fun he had ever been on a date before. I kept trying to work the subject of my engagement into the conversation, but now my doubts about Michael were intensifying. I really did want a mature and stable man—security was important to me—but I just couldn't imagine sacrificing the fun and romance. Now David was showing me that he, too, could be a great deal of fun! What did this mean? Was David really the one I should be with after all?

Just as I was asking myself these questions, David

reached into his pocket and withdrew an engagement ring! "I love you, Sheri, and I want to marry you," he confessed passionately. My head was spinning! David had never said "I love you" to me before. In fact, he told me that he had never said it to *anyone* before! "I've never used those words before, because I only wanted to say 'I love you' to one person." I melted!

"This must be God's way of rescuing me from marrying the wrong person," I thought. "What else could it mean?" So, I said yes. And, no, that wasn't a misprint, I really said yes!

I needed to talk to Susie. I phoned and woke her at 1:00 in the morning. "Uhhh...Susie, I have a problem."

"Sheri Rose, I don't understand you," she said after I had finished telling her the whole story. "You're wasting your time with these guys. Carman is the one for you! How many times do I have to tell you that?"

"Carman's never around," I protested. "We see each other like every three months or something." But Susie didn't waiver, and I was as confused as ever.

So now I was engaged to two men at the same time. I prayed and thought hard about what to do, but my confusion wouldn't subside. Days passed, and Michael and David both tried to reach me by telephone, but I ducked their calls.

Finally, to deal with the stress, I decided to get out of town for awhile. I flew to, you guessed it, San Jose. Kyman was the one guy who never made me feel any kind of pressure. He always seemed to accept me unconditionally. There just wasn't a great deal of "electricity" in our relationship.

During my time in San Jose, Kyman and I went to the beach, worked out together, went out to eat, and had dinner with his grandparents. It was all so very relaxing and stress-free, I never wanted it to end. I had been praying for God's will in the "men" situation, but instead of waiting for His answer, I decided once again to manipulate matters on my own. "Kyman, let me ask you something. If I said I wanted to marry you, would you want to marry me?" No one in their right mind was asking, of course, but Kyman didn't know that, and he said yes. Kyman was *so* easy-going and helpful (we *never* fought), and I *loved* his grandparents. "That's it!" I thought, "I've always wanted to be close to Charlie and Emily, and marrying Kyman would certainly solve that!"

I was beginning to feel comfortable with this idea, and started to think about how I should tell the other guys. Then, suddenly and unexpectedly, Carman called. "How are you, Sheri?"

"Uhhh...fine. How are you?" It was nice to hear from him, but the timing was...well...you know. Next thing I knew, he had invited me to Tulsa for a week. At this point, I thought my brain was going to blow up. What did this mean? Was this God trying to tell me that Susie was right all along? Was my proposal to Kyman just another in a series of huge mistakes? I told Carman I'd come, but only if he promised to give me his undivided attention while I was there (I think what I really needed was the undivided attention of a good therapist!). Carman agreed to my terms, and I flew to Tulsa, leaving my other three suitors in limbo.

I spent five days in Tulsa with Carman, and we had a wonderful time together. Carman seemed to have all the qualities I loved in the other guys all rolled into one. I phoned Susie and told her, "I think you were right. I think he's the one." Of course, I avoided telling Carman about the others.

On our last night together in Tulsa, Carman said to me, "Sheri, I don't want to play any games. We both know why I asked you here."

I gulped. "What do you mean?"

"Well, we're both at an age where we're thinking about who we're going to settle down with, and you know I think you're very special. But...I'm in the middle of an unfinished relationship with someone else, and I don't think it's right to start something new while something else isn't really over yet." I started to cry, not because I was disappointed, but because I felt daggers of guilt stabbing me right through the heart! Three daggers to be exact! Here he was being as honest and as "transparent" with me as he could, and there I was hiding the fact that I was engaged—not to one man, but three!

"I just need to be alone tonight," I told him. I had to be by myself and try to sort out all the confusion. The next day, he drove me to the airport. We were extremely quiet on the way, a little small-talk, but not much else. At the airport, we hugged, and I said goodbye, and headed for home.

Back in San Diego, Susie rebuked me. "You're not trusting in God. Be patient, have faith, and wait for Carman to finish with the others in his life."

"No, Susie, it's over!" I responded.

I quickly felt the urge to do another showcase to keep myself immersed in work. I called Joyce, and we decided to go to San Francisco to produce another event there. Meanwhile, Susie continued to do a great job fielding my phone calls, telling everyone I was out of town and very busy. When they pressed for more details, Susie was mum. But while I was in San Francisco, all the men in my life seemed to simultaneously hit upon the idea of doing an end-run around Susie and calling my dad at his office. Somehow each one managed to get my dad to reveal where I was staying. I then had to tell each "fiancé" something that would explain my behavior, and at this point, I still believed that *anything* would be better than the truth. "I'm sorry, it's just all so overwhelming." Well, *that* much was true. "Marriage is such a huge step, and I'm scared. My parents have had a total of like five divorces over their lifetime, and I just don't ever want to go through that. Please forgive me, but I just need some more time." They all agreed, but they also asked if they could see me. I said no, for now.

Even Peter called me. (Remember the guy I met during aerobics class in Phoenix?) "I wanted to invite you to my 10-year reunion. There's no one else I'd rather bring." Now keep in mind that this guy had *tons* of women. "You know, Sheri," he continued, "someone asked me the other day that if I had to stop all this dating and choose only *one* of the women I know to be my wife, which one would I pick. Well, I know this sounds crazy, 'cause we've only dated a few times, but I said *you*!" At that moment I realized that God surely must have a terrific sense of humor!

"I can't even *begin* to tell you how bad your timing is," I sputtered.

"Pardon me??"

"Oh, look, I'm sorry. It's too hard to explain right now. I...uh...," I hemmed and hawed awhile, and then, believe it or not, I agreed to go with him to his reunion! I'm on the phone with possibly the last breathing male on earth I wasn't already engaged to, and I still couldn't stop myself!

The last night of the showcase arrived. Joyce and I were backstage talking to the 120 or so performers, keeping them calm. I asked if any of them would like me to pray for them, and they all welcomed the idea. Just as I was finishing, Joyce came over to me with a strange look on her face and said,

"You're gonna hafta get down on your knees for *this* one. Maybe even try fasting for awhile."

"What are you talking about?" I inquired.

"Well...could you come over here for a second?" She led me to the curtain and opened it a slit. "Take a look."

"Oh, yeah, great crowd, wonderful turn-out."

"No. Look down," she corrected me.

"Oh, good. All the judges are here. Perfect."

"NO! Look in the first row to the right!" When my eyes moved to the spot she indicated, I thought I was hallucinating—there in the front row, sitting side-by-side, were my three fiancés Kyman, Michael, and David!

"Joyce!" I squealed. "I'm in *huge* trouble!" Of course, I should have thought of that before now. I looked again and saw that each one of them held flowers for me. How could this be happening? As I continued to look, I could see that they were all smiling and were seemingly unaware of one another. They still didn't know! How could I keep them from finding out the hard way? My mind raced—I needed a plan, and I needed one in a hurry. I came up blank. "How am I going to get out of this?" I whimpered to Joyce. "Wait, I know. *You* emcee the show, and *I'll* stay back here!" But she wasn't going for it. "Alright, then you go talk to them one at a time." But she pointed out that there was no way she could talk to one without the others hearing.

I had no choice. I had to start the show, but to say I appeared preoccupied would be a gross understatement. My hands were sweating, my back was sweating, my lips were quivering, and my neck broke out in a rash. I was mispronouncing names of contestants and sponsors, and I forgot to give queues and other stage directions to performers. Toward the end, as I realized the time to face the music was fast approaching, I began hyper-ventilating and had to go backstage to breath into a paper bag. My heart had been beating like a trip-hammer all night, and it was now beginning to hurt. "Maybe I'll have a coronary and won't have to face them!" I thought.

As I stepped back out on stage to wrap things up, I glanced in the direction of the guys for another assessment of the situation. They were still smiling, thank heaven, but at that very moment, Michael turned to the other two and said something along the lines of, "Isn't she gorgeous? That's my girl!" I could see their smiles vanish as they began to compare notes. David shot me a furious look and stormed out. He drove to the airport and got on a plane back to San Diego. Kyman walked off to the side and, as was characteristic for him, waited calmly and politely for me to come to him, but Michael, the fiery one, was in my face immediately at the close of the program.

I had no choice but to come clean, and I explained as best I could. "I'm sorry. I never meant to hurt anyone, but I can't marry you. I really don't think I'm going to marry *anybody* at this point. I should've been more honest with you. I truly do love each of you, but, trust me, you don't want to marry me." Michael left in tears.

I made essentially the same apology to Kyman, then went to the phone to leave a message on David's voice mail. I know that sounds pretty cold, but I wanted him to hear my apology as soon as he checked his messages. I hung up the phone and just stood there for a moment, trying to collect myself. How could I have hurt these men so? Why didn't I have the courage to be honest with them before something like this happened? Why didn't I trust the Lord to guide me in my dating relationships? Finally, all the pressure that had built up found its outlet, and I began to sob deeply.

Joyce had gone up to our room ahead of me, and had prepared a warm bubble bath for me. She also looked up passages in the Bible dealing with God's forgiveness, wrote them on "sticky notes", and posted them on the walls of the bathroom to comfort me. Truly, she was a gift from God—one that I certainly didn't feel I deserved. She never judged me, she just loved me unconditionally. She had tried to encourage me to find a way to tell the truth to the guys sooner, but, in the end, she knew I hadn't meant to hurt anyone. She saw me struggle to turn this final frontier in my life over to God, and she prayed for me and loved me through the whole experience.

As 1986 drew to a close, Joyce and I moved from the Phoenix area to an apartment in San Diego. As Joyce went to be with her family for the holidays, I spent my first Christmas since ninth grade without a boyfriend, but God knew it was time that I learned to lean first and foremost on Him.

Chapter 21

Could This Be The One?

After my escapades with the three wise men (I call them wise because they were smart enough to leave me), I repented to God for being so dishonest with them and made a commitment to trust Him to bring me a godly husband in His good time. Meanwhile, as I was waiting for God to do the matchmaking, I slowly rediscovered some long lost friends—chocolate, ice cream, cheese burgers, fries, chips and dip. I had forgotten how much I loved food and how much it loved me back (me stomach, me thighs...!). My over-indulgence turned into about twenty-five extra pounds.

In January of 1987, I got a call from Michael in Phoenix. My mind flashed for a moment through our turbulent relationship—the fun, the fights, the biblical debates, the on-and-off engagement. Michael called with great news—he had accepted the Lord, Jesus, as his Saviour and wanted to say thanks for introducing him to the truth of God's Word. He also asked if I would come to Phoenix to celebrate his baptism into the faith.

I flew to Phoenix and met Michael and his friend, Kevin, at the airport. Now, you have to understand, after two years of dating Sheri Rose, Best-In-Swimsuit-USA, Michael was more than slightly shocked to see me and my "body by Haagen-Daz" walk off the plane.

"Wow, Sheri!" Michael squinted to make sure it was me.

"Uhh...it's good to see you. We're headed for the health club. Bet you want to come too, huh!" he hinted.

On the way, we stopped off at Kevin's place for a few minutes. I remember thinking as I walked into the house that I didn't *need* to be adored physically, I didn't *care* if I was not a knockout. So what if I was the heaviest I'd been since high school!

Then I stepped through the door and saw Kevin's roommate, Steve, across the room and mentally cursed myself for not being in shape. Steve was the most handsome man I had ever seen! He was a tall, muscular blonde with a warm and gentle smile. Immediately, my senses dulled to all who were around me as I tuned in to his every word and expression as he conversed with someone on the phone. Michael had mentioned something about him in the car—that he was an actor in the middle of filming a movie (Bill and Ted's Excellent Adventure), but what really intrigued me was how he was sharing Jesus with someone on the phone. I responded to his glancing smile and thought, "I could marry someone like that!" I caught myself thinking about the possibility. Here we go again!

Impulsive? I prefer to think of it as a rush of splendid insight! "Could this be the one? Perhaps he likes heavy girls," I wondered. "Fat chance! Maybe I better take Michael up on his offer for a good, hard workout," I decided.

So there I was, at the gym, frantically searching for that one machine that can burn off 20 pounds in 10 minutes. "Uh-oh, Steve walked in! Please God, why does Steve have to be here too?" There I was, self-conscious and confused, fumbling around with the weights, trying to look invisible, when Steve and his marvelous muscles approached.

"You look like you need some help," he said. As I nervously consented to his assistance, I felt my face redden from the unbearable pain of holding my stomach in. I was terribly embarrassed! It was as if I'd never been in a gym before. I couldn't lift anything. I discovered that it's impossible to push ten pounds up when you're trying to suck twenty pounds in!

What is it with me and men? I returned to San Diego and continued to seek the Lord in prayer, Bible study, and church. I didn't want to fall into the same problem all over again! I also spent some more time in the gym because I could not get Steve out of my mind, so I worked out like a maniac hoping I'd see him again soon. Just in case, right?

In May, 1987, Michael called to confirm that I was still taking my showcase winners to L.A. (the dozen or so winners of the previous year's showcases were taken around to personally meet with additional casting directors and agents as part of their winner's prize). Michael mentioned that Steve was going to be in L.A. on that same weekend and would really love to see me there. "Yes!" I yelled as I got off the phone. I couldn't wait.

Steve and I had a great conversation on the phone that week and we realized that we both had the same desire to use our talents for the Lord and share the Gospel with others. Although I didn't mention it to him, I began to think about the possibility of our working together. We agreed to rendezvous when we got to L.A.

My good friend, Anna, knew that something was up from the way I was dieting and working out. I knew that Steve would be getting a lot of attention from everyone else, especially from the girls, and I really wanted to impress him. Even on the set of one of the TV shows we were visiting, one of the actresses there began to pursue him quite openly. I laughed at all the attention Steve was getting, yet thought to myself, "I could never marry an actor!"

I admired Steve's heart for God so much. I vividly remember telling him about my relationships and wondering what kind of girl he would marry. When I asked him about it, he responded that he had made mistakes in dating in the past and had made a covenant with God to not date anyone until He had approved. I couldn't believe this guy hadn't dated *anyone* in over a year! Now, there's discipline.

Steve and I quickly became good friends and I ended up staying a few days longer in L.A. to be with him. I wanted desperately to know more of him and my mind raced for a plan. As we drove down the freeway one night after dinner, I polished my smile and asked, "Steve, I sure could use your help as an emcee on my next showcase in San Jose."

He responded with a pleasant, "Sure, I'd love to", and agreed to fly up after some appointments he had in Los Angeles. I was so excited, I could hardly see straight.

When we met in San Jose, I was in the middle of the showcase and exhausted. Steve came and took a huge load off my shoulders, had all the contestants names memorized, handled many of the unforeseen details, and got a lot of attention from the girls. He didn't seem to notice all his admirers, he was so focused on helping me produce a professional event. "I think I'm falling in love!"

Steve was everything I wasn't. He was calm and rational, noticed details, spoke only carefully chosen words, and seemed unaffected by any limelight. He'd been raised by godly parents who loved him unconditionally, so playing emotional games was absolutely foreign to him. His needs were simple; his convictions were strong. I, on the other hand, had passion like a ship at sea! My sails blown by gusts of emotion that swirled and shifted with every circumstance.

It seemed I *never* lacked for words. Compared to Steve's concise thoughts, mine showered down and flooded a conversation. I talked all the time and usually had no idea what I was saying! Whatever it was, though, it seemed the spotlight always found it's way to me. "Could I attract the same attention from Steve?" I wondered.

After the San Jose Showcase, Steve was in a hurry to get back to Phoenix to work on a play he was writing, producing and performing with his friend, Martin. I had to act fast! What else was new?

The two of us went on a long walk that night and talked about lots of spiritual things. I was still a baby Christian and loved to hear Steve share his knowledge about the Christian life and God's forgiveness. It made perfect sense that God had a plan for me and called me to serve Him and minister to others. "Exactly like Charlie and Emily!" I thought to myself. Steve and I also talked about how great it was to see God work in the lives of these actors and models and that we both felt lead to minister to them. By the end of that night, Steve and I were in perfect agreement. We would team up to produce the next showcase in Sacramento! I was ecstatic! I would have the entire month of July with my dream man!

By this time, I was back staying with Scott and Anna Ruiz, my friends in San Jose. I knew in my heart that Steve and I were a *perfect* team and that he really must be "The One". I even told the women at the health club that, "I think I met the man I'm going to marry!" They knew I was serious when they saw me work out like an animal.

When Steve flew back into town, I was ready! As I headed out the door to meet Steve at the airport, Scott and Anna took one look at my sleeveless, form fitting cotton dress outfit and pleaded with me not to put Steve through any *unnecessary* temptations "Unnecessary? I want him to *want* me," I thought. "What's more *necessary* than that?" I wasn't in the mood for a lecture from "mom and dad" so, off I went with hook fully baited.

To my surprise, Steve's response to my eye-batting, dimple-polishing, sexy-dress greeting was, "Say, you look really nice today." I was crushed.

"This is a *serious* problem if this big oaf isn't even raising one romantically-inclined, semi-interested eyebrow!" He just did *not* adore me the way I wanted him to, and he didn't try to sweep me off my feet the way I always dreamt would happen when I met Mr. Right. He had never so much as held my hand, let alone discussed marriage, or even dating! He always remained a perfect gentleman. This made me love him all the more!

It was the Fourth of July, and I was in LOVE, but there were still no fireworks! It was time to kick my mission into high gear. I was already used to getting up at 4:00 a.m. to get my hair and makeup perfect for my breakfast meeting with Steve every morning. So, I polished my dimples some more (haven't I done that enough!), glued on fake eyelashes, turned up the smiles a notch or two, sprayed a few extra shots of perfume and I even managed a few extra laughs at his jokes. Well, one or more of the above must have worked because we shared a wonderfully romantic evening watching the fireworks and added to the splendor by sharing our first kiss! That night, I slow danced on his feet and swam in his eyes. When we said good night, we hugged like two friends who had known each other for years.

I soon realized that the victory was definitely not yet *in the bag.* Steve apparently was not so hasty about committing himself to me and encouraged us to stay *friends* in the Lord first. I hated that! Just when you finally *want* a guy to pull out a ring, he wants to stay *friends!* How dare he! So, I tried even harder to manipulate him and even acted helpless in situations that I was perfectly capable of handling myself.

He wasn't fooled and it prompted him to respond, "You know, if you want me to do something, all you have to do is ask." He was so uncomplicated and so unmoved by all my manipulation that it made me crazy.

Steve and I had been praying together every day and the more time we spent in the Word, the more I understood that our relationship needed to be based on a spiritual foundation or nothing at all. It took me a while to realize that my own tricks would only bring trouble. I finally turned to the most powerful weapon I had—prayer. I prayed earnestly for God to move in Steve's heart and our relationship. I loved Steve deeply and promised God that I'd let go so *His* will could be done. It was hard to step out of the way, but I knew it was right.

It was near the end of July with only a few days left in the showcase, and even though we were having an incredible time together, it still seemed as though a veil was over Steve's heart. "Does he even love me?" I questioned.

That night, Steve took me to a nice dinner. We both poked at our food nervously as we acknowledged the few remaining days and hours together. My plans were to take a few months off, move into the girls dorms at BIOLA (Bible Institute of Los Angeles in La Mirada) University and surround myself with godly Christian girls and Bible study while auditing some courses. I wanted badly to mature as a Christian.

Steve's plans were to—well we knew all along that he felt called to Hollywood to use his acting talents for God (Lord knows that industry needs some godly people). Then, out of the blue, as if Steve had suddenly picked up another script, he looked me in the eyes and asked, "How would you feel about me not moving to L.A.? What I mean is, how would you feel about me moving down near BIOLA, near you?"

I could feel my knees knock and the lump in my throat barely push out my response, "Uh, would you excuse me a moment?" I got up, staggered to the bathroom, grabbed the nearest lady available and shrieked, "I met the man I'm going to marry, and I think he's about to propose and...," I stammered on, with intermittent shrieks of joy that stunned all the ladies room inhabitants and especially my unfortunate captive.

"Uh, Great! Good for you...uhh...I'm very...we're all very happy for you," she stuttered as she and the others cautiously backed out the door or retreated to the nearest stall.

I managed to compose myself and returned to the table. I knew that there was no way that Steve could pursue his acting career and live that far away from Hollywood. Something was up. "Okay...why?" I asked Steve.

He leaned forward and held both my hands in his. I could tell he lacked his usual composure. "Well," he stuttered, "you know there is an excellent seminary there at BIOLA and I've always wanted to continue my education...." he paused. "The truth is Sheri, I just can't picture spending the rest of my life without you in it."

My eyes immediately filled with tears of joy as time seemed suspended for the next several minutes. As if in a dream, our surroundings blurred as we gazed passionately at each other. Steve's eyes glistened with tears as he grinned from ear to ear. "I feel just like a veil has suddenly been lifted from my eyes!" Steve was almost laughing now, as he boyishly placed his fingers on the pulse of his neck. "I'm so madly in love with you that I can't keep my heart from racing. Feel my pulse! Go on, feel it!" We both laughed ...over two plates of untouched food.

On the way back to the hotel that night, I thought to myself, "You know, he never did actually propose to me!" I was afraid to say anything. When we arrived, Steve did something a little peculiar. He asked me to go to my room for half an hour and seek the Lord in His Word and in prayer. As I did, my heart was flooding with emotions as I thanked God and begged Him for His will to be done and not mine. I didn't want to make any more mistakes.

Steve knocked on the door, smiled like he was up to something, and took me by the hand to his room. All the lights were out except for two candles on a small table in the middle of the room, between them was a third candle that was unlit. He then had us kneel down next to the table facing each other with hands clasped.

"Have you ever had communion?" he asked.

I shook my head, no, daring not to let our gaze part.

Steve then broke bread and took a cup of grape juice and explained the sacrifice Jesus made for us so that we could be made a part of God's family. He explained the significance of the blood and the covenant God had made with man throughout history and, because we rejected Him, He made a final covenant through His son, Jesus. That night, I had my first communion and understood what Jesus really did for me as the

Passover Lamb.

Steve then took both my hands, bowed his head and prayed for God's guidance in our relationship and asked for God's blessing as he sought to join our lives together. My heart raced as I thought about it. After the prayer, our eyes then met as he asked the question that I *knew* was from the Lord. He sought something that only now was I finally ready and able to give—my heart, for life, in marriage!

Steven Gene Shepherd, the man of my dreams! The only thing more gorgeous than his body, is his heart!

It's about time this guy kissed me! I worked hard enough!

Communion by Candelight! Steve made that night incredibly romantic. He thought of everything, even his camera and tripod!

On stage at the Sacramento Showcase when we announced our engagement to the 100 contestants. They bought us beautiful wedding bears to remember them by.

Chapter 22

Meeting the Inlaws

Steve and I were so excited about what God was doing in our lives. We announced our engagement to all the contestants at the showcase and then immediately went for the phones to call home. Steve decided to wait and "spring" me as a surprise at his grandparents 50th anniversary in North Dakota the following week. I, on the other hand, winced as I dialed the oh, so familiar numbers to home. Even though I knew God had spoken, sometimes Susie was listening somewhere else.

"Are you sure, Rosie?" she said. "What about Carman?" I responded with resounding conviction, "Steve's the *one* and I have no doubt." It felt good to know. I can't explain it, I just *knew*, and there was peace in that. Dad, on the other hand, jumped on a plane and flew up to the showcase right away. Steve didn't know Dad well enough to be nervous (Fortunately, Steve had missed out on those chapters of my life). To my surprise, Dad and Steve hit it off fantastically.

Dad pulled me aside right before the show. "He's genuine, Sheri. I like him."

Steve approached us, dressed in his tux for the show, placed his hand on Dad's shoulder and asked, "Phil, can I ask you something?"

"Here goes....!" I thought. Steve hasn't done the traditional "Can I have your daughter's hand?" speech.

Steve continued, "The show's about to start and I have no black socks. Can I borrow yours?"

For one brief, breath-taking moment, I looked anxiously at Dad and then at Steve. Then suddenly, my dad busted up in hysterical laughter. He reached down and tore off his shoes and bequeathed his own socks to his new son-in-law-to-be.

Now it was my turn to meet the inlaws. I had enough trouble with *blood* relatives, who knew what would happen with these strangers. I was hopeful, however, and Steve assured me that we'd get along great. His two sisters were school teachers, his mom was a school librarian, and his dad was a high school principal. What makes him think I could possibly get along with a family like that? The only part of school that got along with *me* was recess and lunch! I could just see it now—I would have my grammar corrected, have homework assigned, be told to "Hush!" and get sent to the principal without ever leaving the family! (I suppose gum-chewing at the wedding is out of the question!)

Steve and I were to rendezvous in Minneapolis and meet his sister, Susan and her fiancé. We would then connect to Bismark, meet Mom and Dad, drive two hours to Uncle Roy's farm and attend the huge gala anniversary celebration for his grandparents that weekend.

Now, you have to remember that I'm a southern California city girl and always have been. When Steve said we were spending the weekend at his uncle's farm, somehow, in my mind, the word "farm" was translated into a sprawling, palatial estate in the country complete with convertible Mercedes, elegant parties, beautifully radiant people, you know —like "Dallas". So, I arrayed myself with such splendid attire to make Bobby Ewing fall off his horse! Anyway, when Steve met me at the airport in Minneapolis, I was wearing a designer fleece jumpsuit, embroidered with rhinestones, with silver high heels, accessorized with rhinestone earrings, jewelry, curled hair, manicured nails, false eyelashes, and the maximum amount of makeup allowed by law. I figured if I could send the metal detectors at the airport into a tizzy, I ought to be able to have a good showing for all of Steve's family.

Unfortunately, my darling Steven did not share my excitement or flair for fashion. "Uh...It's very nice honey. Umm...now you know we're going to a F-A-R-M, right?"

"Oh sure, I can't wait to meet everyone!" I replied, completely missing the subtle hint.

He tried again, "Umm...I'm not sure if you're going to be comfortable in that, especially since we have to ride in the back of a truck for two hours to get there."

Just then, Steve's sister, Susan, strolled up clad in jeans and a T-shirt. She took one look at me and blurted, "You look like you walked off the cover of Vogue Magazine or something. You're going to a farm, you know." Then she belched.

Well, being the people-pleaser that I am, I took a mental note, "Rhinestones are 'out'—belches are 'in'." So, I went into the restroom to change into something somewhere between dazzling and frumpy and emerged wearing cute sweats with matching peach tennis shoes.

Susan tried to keep from rolling her eyes, "Oh...much better," she mumbled.

I know when I met the rest of the family, I was probably quite a shock (the first of many, I'm sure!). When I met Steve's mom, though, she cried and hugged me tightly. To her, you see, I was the damsel rescuing the shining knight from the snare of Hollywood. She had been praying fervently for God to bring her son a wife. I loved my new "mom" immediately. It's fun to be someone's answer to prayer.

I handed Steve's dad a card I had written on the way there, thanking them and God for the tremendous impact their son had made on my life. Steve's father sat there in the airport smiling as he read, shedding the only tear Steve had ever seen from him. (He was probably dumfounded that a human adult could have such tragic grammar and spelling!) I am painfully aware that many primates have better handwriting than I do. Just look at one of my autographed photos if you don't believe me!

After piling seven of us into their Landcruiser (Steve and I were stowed in back with the luggage) and driving for two hours, we arrived at his uncle's beautiful farm. Once I de-glamorized, I thoroughly enjoyed a wonderful weekend with Steve's gracious and loving family-to-be.

My new Inlaws...preparing me for "roughing it" on a camping trip. I thought "roughing it" meant a hotel without room service.

All of Steve's family at Cousin Nicole's wedding in North Dakota. Steve and I were producing a showcase somewhere else, and missed the fun.

Chapter 23

The Whirlwind Wedding

The next two months, our whirlwind courtship turned into a whirlwind engagement. We were tossed about in a sea of emotional and physical changes. This was nothing new to me—my life was always in turmoil, but it was a bumpy ride for Steve, and he just hung on tight and kept a cool head.

July 31st, we were engaged in Sacramento. We then journeyed immediately to the heartland of North Dakota. Steve flew back to Phoenix to spend three straight all-nighters to prepare for and perform in a play with his friend, Martin. I jetted back to Sacramento to cleanup the loose ends of our showcase. I hopped back on a plane to Phoenix to see Steve's performance. We then drove all night to pick up my car in San Diego, moved to Fullerton, got an apartment and enrolled Steve in Seminary. Whew! How much more could we fit into three weeks? Oh yeah—what about the wedding?

Steve and I nixed the typical six month engagement in favor of the quick-and-to-the-point route. Were we impatient? Yes! But, also practical. We couldn't afford two rents in L.A. and knew nobody in town. Steve's sister already had a Christmas wedding planned, and we couldn't wait until next summer. What's the big deal, we thought, we produced huge showcases, how hard could it be to produce a little wedding? We felt that three weeks was more than enough time to inform family and friends and whip it together. (Caution! Kids, don't try this at home!).

An important thing to remember is that we felt strongly the hand of God shuffling us along from the day we met all the way to the altar. As our October 3, 1987 wedding day approached, Steve was extremely busy with his graduate courses and I was staying with a friend, so naturally there were chapters in my life that I hadn't gotten around to sharing with my new husband-to-be. It'll have to wait until after the wedding— no big deal. So needless to say, word started spreading that Sheri Rose, a.k.a."The Destroyer" was finally tying the knot.

"No, really? Sheri Rose is getting hitched?"

"You're kidding! To who? Steve? Steve who?"

"Which one is he?"

"Yeah, right! I'll believe it when I see it!"

In three weeks time, we managed to throw together quite a production. We were married in the campus chapel at BIOLA under the glare of television lights. The three TV-quality cameras we got, thanks to my dad, captured an interesting mixture of wedding guests—my dad and the Jewish relatives, Mom and her parents, Susie, my stepmom, Steve's family and seminary classmates, past showcase contestants and our Hollywood casting director and agent friends. Oh, did I mention that Kyman and Michael were both there!

What a wedding ceremony! My 18 month old niece screamed her lungs out; the temperature outside was 107 degrees (a record in L.A.); Joyce cried her eyes out as she sang *Friends are Friends Forever*; and, to top it all off, God gave us a stamp of approval with a hearty 5.1 earthquake. Altogether, it was a screamin', sizzlin', cryin', earth shakin' good time!

Our honeymoon was uneventful. Just kidding! God

truly blesses a relationship that *waits* for marriage (Kids, *do* try this at home!). After a fun-filled, romantic two days in Newport Beach, things kicked back into high gear. Steve had five mid-terms that week and then we went immediately into an L.A. trip where we had flown in the winners of our past two showcases to do the Hollywood agent tour thing. Naturally, this kind of pressure was bound to lead to our first *misunderstanding*.

Oh, I had already noticed a few *differences* between us. For one thing, it became clear that Steve had expected a more down-to-earth girl. Once, while on one of our many long drives, Steve pulled into a service station.

"You get the windows, while I fill the tank," he quipped as he hopped out of the car.

"Excuse me?" I laughed in disbelief. "You must be joking. Get what?"

"You know, the *bugs*...would you mind washing the windows?" he continued, ever so politely.

Well, I had never even pumped my own gas before, let alone engaged in any sort of insect removal. I stubbornly remained in the car. "Obviously, this one needs some training," I thought. Looking back, I'm sure he was probably thinking the same thing about me!

Upon moving into our new apartment, we knew we needed to pick up a few necessities at the local department store since all we had were the clothes on our backs. Steve eagerly agreed, so we waltzed out the door, hand-in-hand. Once at the store, I skipped along impulsively snatching up the first thing that caught my eye (remember, I used to think nothing of spending $5,000 on a shopping spree when I was single).

"Ooh, that's nice!"..."Wow! That's cute"..."I think we need

two of those, don't we Steven dear?"   I turned around and noticed that my new husband, who, only minutes before had bounced into the store vibrantly alive, was now a quivering, pale, basket-case. His eyes were glassy and he mumbled unintelligibly as his shaky fingers nervously searched for his pulse. I broke my shopping stride long enough to comfort him, "There, there, honey. Don't worry, we really do *need* all this stuff." One hour and seven hundred and ninety-one dollars later, he nearly exploded in a nervous fit. Obviously, this man was not born to shop!

*Our wedding picture from October 3, 1987.
I had it blown up poster-size, framed, and
hung in our bedroom as a huge reminder
of a wonderful day!*

Chapter 24

It's Time To Settle Down

After a Showcase in Modesto over Christmas break in 1987, we were excited to finally be able to take a real honeymoon in beautiful Lake Tahoe. I had all my designer ski wear, matching boots, earrings, sunglasses and couldn't wait to hit the slopes. Unfortunately, instead of my dream ski vacation with my husband, I was so nauseous, I ended up hugging a toilet in the lodge. As I was getting acquainted with one particular toilet in stall number two, I was startled to hear what sounded like an echo coming from stall number one. It turned out to be another helpless woman sharing my miserable condition.

"You got the flu too?" I inquired compassionately as we both rinsed and spit.

"Nah," she responded. "I'm pregnant again."

I then began comparing symptoms with this obviously experienced mother and discovered that I might have come down with a severe case of pregnancy! I muttered a queasy, "Thank you," and staggered out the door to find Steve.

"Quick, you have to buy me a pregnancy tester," I informed him.

"Why would you think you need a pregnancy test?" he wanted to know.

"Because I met a woman in the rest room who was

throwing up, and she's pregnant," I replied.

"Sheri, that's not how you get pregnant," Steve teased. "It's not contagious, you know." Back at the hotel, we discovered that our lives were in for a radical change (babies do that!) and that no amount of birth control can stop God.

On the long ride home from the mountains of Tahoe, I tried to imagine what it would be like to be a mother. I recalled the check list I had made of the twenty things I had planned to accomplish before holding my firstborn in my arms. As we bounced down the highway, I couldn't think of *one* thing on my "Before Motherhood List" that I could cross off. Oh, wait, there was one—I got married!

After I returned home and went to the doctor, he said that I had one of the worst cases of morning sickness that he had ever seen. I was severely dehydrated and in and out of the hospital during the first five months of my pregnancy but, fortunately, as my stomach filled out, the morning sickness let up.

Even though the pregnancy was hard, I was really looking forward to settling down for the first time in my life in a somewhat normal family environment. As I thought about where I would like to raise a family, I couldn't get Steve's parents off my mind. I would move anywhere to be near them. Steve was shocked that his California girl was willing to move to Arizona in the summer.

In August, we made the big move to Scottsdale. I was so excited about moving into our new house. I didn't realize that it was 120 degrees outside until I walked out to the driveway and my rubber thongs stuck to the concrete. What was I thinking? It was August, and I was nine months pregnant. I must have been insane not to wait until the summer had ended. I've never been so hot and miserable in my life! If you've never been to Arizona during the summer, put this book down, go into your bathroom, plug in your blow dryer, turn it on *high*, and stick it in your mouth. Now you know exactly what an Arizona summer feels like (Don't forget, it's a dry heat!). Now, before anyone from the Arizona Chamber of Commerce decides to write me a nasty letter, let me point out that we now live in Phoenix year round and LOVE it!

Chapter 25

Mother to Mother

As summer sizzled by, and the birth of our new baby grew near, I sometimes doubted if I was even capable of being the type of mother our new son would need. In my quiet time, I couldn't help but think about my relationship with my own mother and what a constant fight it was just to be close to her. I remember longing for her approval and affection. Now that I'm older, I realize that I too, made many mistakes with her. I prayed that God would somehow erase the pain of our past and reconcile us to be the mother and daughter that He intended us to be. I knew that forgiveness is the first step to inner healing, and "just as God has forgiven us, we are to forgive each other".

As I continued to pray, God laid on my heart to call my mother on the phone and tell her that I loved her and that I wanted her to be a part of my life. Just as I was getting brave enough to call, I received a letter from her. Before I opened the letter I anticipated a love note or a *Congratulations* on my pregnancy. Maybe even some words of wisdom. But I never dreamed that my mother would write accusing me of being responsible for every family problem that we had ever had. She said that I was self-centered and had disrupted her life. Enclosed with the letter were all my baby pictures and my baby book. She said she wanted to forget me forever. I was devastated.

As I sat there and cried my eyes out and had my own personal pity party, I started to realize how Jesus had been falsely accused. Steve and I prayed and this gave me the strength to write her a letter back and ask her to forgive me for everything that she had accused me of doing. Two weeks later, I received a phone call from her. "Sheri, this is Mom. I want you to know that I'd like to have you back in my life again."

I immediately started to cry. "Mom, I need you. I've always needed you. Let's get to know each other." I knew God had answered my prayer and I was finally free!

The time finally came for us to deliver our baby. I knew that no one was going to give me a certificate from the "Grunt and Push School of Natural Childbirth" so, I opted for the less-than-heroic method—I begged for drugs! My goal, like all women I know, was to get through this childbirth as quickly and painlessly as possible.

My husband hung in there with me the whole time. "Here I am at your *cervix*, Honey," he would joke.

After twenty hours of labor, my doctor started yelling four letter words at me.

"P-U-S-H, Sheri!" He yelled.

"Me push?" I yelled back. "Why do I have to push? You're the one with the salad spoons! Why don't you just *pull* the baby out and get it over with!"

Finally, the ordeal was over and the doctor announced, "It's a beautiful baby boy! Ohh... he looks just like grandpa Phil!"

"He'll snap out of it," assured Steve, "...I hope!"

I'm sure that my dad loved being told that his face looked like a puffy red, squished-up conehead!

As we brought home our precious little Jacob Andrew, I was flooded with emotions. Steve could sense my anxiety and said, "Just pretend that you're baby sitting."

"But, I've never baby sat before!" I cried.

"Oh. Well, Jacob's never had a mommy before, so you're both starting from scratch," he said lovingly.

For as long as I could remember, I held on desperately to an image of a loving family I never had. That night, as little Jacob lay peacefully sleeping, I sat motionless at his side. My eyes were glassy with tears. My heart ached with an intense love—a love I didn't know I was capable of having—a love I guess only mommies can know, yet sadly, a love not all mommies know how to express. I thought, "Does my little Jacob *know* I love him?" I reached to his side and wriggled my finger into the grip of his tiny hand. I imagined the countless times in years ahead that he would reach out with that very same hand and say, "Love me, mommy! Love me." Oh, his tiny lips may never form those exact words, but, if he's anything like me, it's the heart that does the asking.

In the coming weeks, I developed an intense resolve to *show* little Jacob the love I know he needed. Looking back on my life, I remembered all the conditions that were placed on loving and being loved. I had never learned how to give or receive it because I thought all along that love was an emotion you shared or denied, depending on how you felt at the moment. That kind of love, sooner or later, always fails. With my new husband and son, I was determined to break the curse of "failed" love that had plagued my past.

9 months pregnant and about to explode. I made Steve take me 4-wheeling to speed up the labor!

Proud Daddy holding his baby, Jacob, for the very first time. Sept. 15, 1988

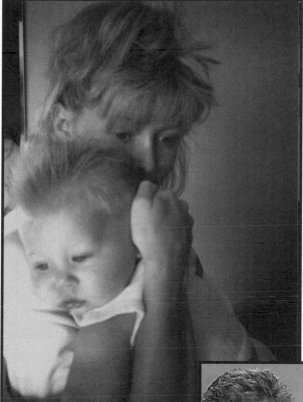

I remember holding my baby son and praying that God would give me wisdom. I wanted so much to be a good mom for him.

Our Christmas Family Photo, 1989

Chapter 26

What's Next?

As we began our new family life in Arizona, Steve enrolled at Western Seminary and started job hunting. He contacted people in several ministries and churches as well as people in broadcasting and in productions. He also touched base with his agent locally about resuming his modeling and acting. Now, my husband is a college graduate, extremely talented, and works well with others. But, no matter how many resumés he sent out and phone calls he made to try to get work, nothing happened. He could hardly get an interview! We knew from past experiences with the Lord that when He closes a door that tightly, He is trying to get our attention.

When Steve and I got engaged, we knew that God called us together to minister the Gospel. As we prayed, we both felt strongly that we were being led to go back to producing showcases and minister to actors, models, and singers. I must admit that I was not thrilled about traveling again, and Steve was really loving school, but deep inside, we knew that God's plan was far greater than our own, and that He cares more about our character than our comfort.

As we made plans, God went before us and opened up many doors. As we continued, we were able to build friendships with many Hollywood industry executives who willingly shared their time and expertise at our showcases all around the country.

Thousands auditioned to be in our showcases because of the opportunity to meet highly respected casting directors with casting credits that included: MGM, Family Matters, Lorimar Television, The Young and the Restless, Warner Brothers, Beverly Hills 90210, Melrose Place, Twin Peaks, and many others. They were also able to meet top agents and managers scouting talent for industry elite such as LA Models Agency, William Morris Agency, and Star Search.

We even produced showcases in Los Angeles and brought in the winners from our showcases around the country. In L.A., showcases are a dime-a-dozen, and having one or two working casting directors or agents in attendance is a major accomplishment. Our first show in L.A. drew more than one hundred industry professionals (producers, agents, casting directors, managers) who were all there to see the talent we had discovered. The real success was that we had more than one hundred requests for interviews and auditions for the actors, models and vocalists we brought. It felt great to have that kind of positive attention in a tough place like Los Angeles.

Even more gratifying than helping young performers realize their dreams of signing with an agent or getting cast in a TV show or movie, we loved watching people overcome incredible obstacles and grow personally and spiritually. We saw hundreds of changed lives. Addictions were broken, families were restored and many times people discovered the pursuit of Hollywood did not hold the answer after all.

One young man had abandoned his wife, his family, and even his job as a youth pastor in search of that golden dream of Hollywood. He confessed that our showcase was the last place that he expected to hear about Jesus. This prodigal was reminded that life is about commitment to God and others. He thanked us and promptly returned to his family.

Over the years, Steve and I have kept and cherished hundreds of cards and letters that reflect that kind of personal growth. We saw our showcases as a present, beautifully wrapped with the enticing glamour of Hollywood. We hoped, however, as thousands tore off the wrapping, they would discover what was inside would prove to be far more precious in the long run.

We realize that many people looked at our showcases, our lifestyle, and even our marriage and thought, "What a perfect little package! Look at Sheri. She has such a glamorous life traveling here and there, hob-knobbing with Hollywood elite, working with her handsome husband, making a good living. Must be nice!"

Our goal was to be upbeat and positive and have our act together as we worked with hundreds of different personalities at a time. This gave us an image of success, but only our staff knew the "behind-the-scenes". The truth is that it was one difficult battle after another in a seven year war. There were many victories, but also numerous failures. Any one doing work for the Lord knows that the battle is in a spiritual realm and the enemy is often not seen.

Our loving, hardworking staff who saw behind the scenes and hung with us. Joyce, Patti, Krista, Ryan, Rebecca, Jodie, Stacey and, of course, Steve, Jacob, and Sheri.

Over 150 beautiful contestants in our first Miss Arizona USA and Miss Arizona Teen USA Preliminary Pageant!

Chapter 27

Stop the World I-Want to Get Off!

Steve and I could tell when something great was about to happen for God. His victories are often preceded by a spiritual attack from the enemy. Because we are both stubborn personalities and have basically night and day backgrounds and temperaments, our marriage usually has a huge bulls-eye painted on it. It seems like our relationship is always the target of attack.

We struggled often with our roles in running the business. I was an amazing quick-change artist. Without even noticing, I'd be a loving, child-like sweetheart one minute and a "take no prisoners—we're doing it *my* way or not at all" the next minute. Steve, likewise, couldn't decide whether to be charming and funny or the much less popular, "Mr. Correction-A-Minute Bossy Pants." His well-meaning *fathering* drove me berserk!

One of our more memorable *pre-game* fights was a sight to behold. The day before a showcase in the Bay Area in California, we got into a heated *discussion*. If there's one thing I knew how to do growing up, it's how to fight. Steve was clueless—he obviously needed some lessons in losing his temper. His calm, stubborn retorts would drive me crazy!

"Why don't you show some emotion!" I screamed. I knew I was getting somewhere as steam started rising out of his ears. The next thing I knew, there was a huge crash.

In a flagrant display of pent-up emotional fireworks, Steve had kicked in the mirrored closet door. I gasped. The door shattered. Steve winced in pain.

"Now, if that's not enough emotion for you... I think I could probably work up a good cry," he threatened as his rapidly swelling toe began popping the seams in his shoe.

"Wow! What an emotional performance!" I thought. "He sure learns quick!"

The next morning we had to get up at the crack of dawn and get to the airport. We had seven hundred pounds of computer equipment plus our luggage *and* a nine month old baby, whom I couldn't even carry because I awoke with a most horrendous case of food poisoning. I begged for a wheelchair, sat my son on my lap and slung our computer over the back as my husband limped along on his battered foot, piloting this laughable mess of a family through the airport.

It seemed that before, during, and after every showcase, I wanted to quit. The stress was incredibly hard on our marriage and family, but, by now, we had office overhead and a staff that depended on us. I'd often pray, "Lord, I want a home. A real one, like regular people." Each time the answer seemed to be, "Not yet!" Steve and I would often talk about other options and even tried some things on the side, but it seemed like the showcases were the wisest thing to do with our talents and the contacts we had been blessed with.

Now-a-days everybody, it seems, produced showcases and model searches, but when I got started, they were extremely rare. One of our biggest competitors did only two showcases a year and they were wildly profitable. They knew that we had a growing influence in the industry and offered us a deal where we would work in conjunction with their large association.

They had taken a great liking to us personally and, although they didn't share our desire to spread the Gospel, we decided to give them a fair shot on our next showcase.

We had grown accustomed to coming into a city and overwhelming the population with the incredible opportunity to meet with Hollywood's best career-makers, get professional photos, workshops and training for under $400. In one city, we auditioned more than 1,500 people in one day to be in our show! Well, needless to say, our little operation of bringing Hollywood to town totally wiped out the market for local modeling schools and others who profited by sending kids and their $3,000 to our competitor's showcase. We soon became national targets of a "Let's put them out of business and eliminate the competition" campaign.

On our next showcase, we had more than 500 people audition. Unfortunately, as those who were selected to be in the show came back for their first orientation, they were met just outside the hotel entrance by an individual posing as an agent for the Attorney General's office. As he passed out business cards (Xerox copies of a real agent's card!) he flagrantly accused us of running a scam and told our contestants that we were under investigation. Of course, none of this was remotely true, but the damage was done (We later discovered that he had been hired by a local modeling school, who felt threatened by our presence in their town). Many of our would-be contestants got scared and left—no longer willing to trust us with their money. I remember fighting back the tears many times, but we knew that the show must go on (and it did!) regardless of our personal and financial loss. None of the contestants knew it, but we went deeply in debt from this show.

After this disaster, we were forced to go immediately to another showcase to catch-up financially. Again, we were met with additional slander and went even further into debt. This time we really *were* investigated by the Attorney General's Office. Fortunately, after observing us and our week long production, the investigator loved what we were doing and filed a very favorable report.

It got increasingly frustrating to battle slander and rumors that started forming even before we reached a new city. People just did not realize that the impressive list of industry professionals we were bringing to each show would never have put their names on our advertising or continue to come to our shows if we had even a hint of scam on us.

The next big blow was not only personally slanderous, but our lawyer said it would provide us with the final piece that would seal our ability to win an Anti-trust suit if we wished to pursue it. Letters were turning up all over the country that were distributed by this competitor to hundreds of affiliated modeling schools and agencies and to all their students and clients. Steve and I were listed personally on what they called a "Beware List" and we were basically lumped in with other scams to watch out for.

So why didn't we sue them? They're worth millions after all. As painful as it was, we knew that it would be more painful and stressful to file a law suit and involve innocent contestants in a two year—or longer—battle. We trusted that the Lord would provide for our needs in a less destructive manner.

After six years, it seemed that things were getting harder and harder. We tried to keep a spiritual perspective on the showcases, but Steve and I were having increasingly more trouble working together. We looked at each other as business partners and not as friends or lovers. The added strain of keeping staff paid and the office running took all the fun out of it. Often the sparks our marriage needed were so few and far between that I began to resent Steve and this big monster of a company that we had to keep feeding.

In 1993, I was offered the directorship of the Miss Arizona USA and Miss Arizona Teen USA as well as the Mrs. Arizona United States Pageants. I love working with young girls and women, so I excepted the offers hoping that this would be a way for me to simplify my life, stop traveling, and have more hours to spend at home. What was I thinking? I can't do *anything* simple. I made wildly ambitious plans to give these girls the time of their lives. I found a sponsor who would pay for the very expensive TV coverage and planned a full-blown televised production. At the last minute, the sponsor backed out and left us to try and pay the bills, knowing that we had to continue the show even though our funds were depleted. The pageant turned out beautifully and all the girls were treated like queens, but unfortunately, we went even further into debt because of the loss of the sponsor and we had to let our pageant staff go. Again, the stress was building in our home life and Steve and I were fighting again. "We have to stop working together!" I would cry to Steve. "Can't you just get a job or something?"

"I would," he'd lash back, "but I'm too busy working for you!"

My dear friend and business manager, Lana, was not only my right hand while producing the pageant events, she was my counselor—a crutch of good judgement when my senses went limp (which was quite often). She pleaded with me to listen to reason.

"You and Steve are bringing out the very worst in each other." I had heard it before and I knew she was right. If something didn't change soon, our marriage would be history. Steve agreed. He didn't want to be business partners any more than I did.

Unfortunately, it wasn't going to be easy to make this transition. We still had winners from our past showcases who had won a trip to go to Hollywood to meet and audition with casting directors and agents. Also, our staff was depending on us to pay the salaries we owed them from the past showcase.

In Steve's attempt to save the integrity of our company, he teamed up with a co-producer—a well respected personal manager from Nashville. They made plans to direct their next two showcases in San Francisco and Nashville. If they were successful, we would not only be able to get out of debt, we'd have enough to last us for a few months. They put together the most elite panel of casting directors and agents to participate I had ever seen. But, for whatever reason, God was closing this door completely. Our once popular showcases had lost their appeal and Nashville was the final straw. We lost another $20,000 and were unable to pay the staff and the vendors all that we owed.

Creditors began harassing us daily and we could see no way to come out of this downward spiral. To top it all off, I found out that I was pregnant again. How could I possibly take care of another baby, when I barely had time for Jacob, and where were we going to find the money for this pregnancy and birth? *I had to get off of this insane roller coaster ride!*

Chapter 28

Could Things Get Any Worse?

Steve was taking all of this very hard and I knew he felt like a failure. I wanted so badly to be a comfort to my husband, but I was so burned-out with so many things falling apart in my life, that I didn't know where to begin. We both wanted desperately to figure out a way to shut down the production company without hurting anybody. We knew staff members were angry at us because they needed to pay their personal bills and we still owed them money. Our bank account was overdrawn, our mortgage was late and, in the midst of all the stress, I miscarried our baby. I even sold my wedding ring so that we could have groceries.

I also knew that I didn't have the strength or the funds to keep producing the Arizona Pageants. But, how could I tell the 100 precious young girls who looked up to me as a role model, that their director had no choice but to quit. It was so humiliating to let them down!

It seemed like Steve and I were fighting constantly and I felt like it was a huge mistake that we had ever become business partners. I constantly felt like a failure as a wife and mother. I was so exhausted from worry and stress that I was getting sick all the time and I could feel my body starting to deteriorate. If something didn't change soon, I was going to explode! During one of my pageant orientations, I actually passed out while I was speaking. My business manager, Lana, took me to the hospital that evening and I was diagnosed with Chronic Fatigue Syndrome and acute anemia.

The stress in my life caused my once positive outlook on life to change drastically. I had nothing left to give and felt like no one could possibly understand what I was going through. Almost everyone, it seemed, had judgmental words of criticism, and very little compassion. I was so overwhelmed that I started resenting all the people who were depending on me, including staff, pageant contestants, showcase winners, and even my family. Finally, we had no choice but to declare bankruptcy. We both felt like complete failures and there was absolutely nothing we could do about it.

Our dear friends, Mark and Leslie Bundy, came to our rescue. Leslie is a godly wife and mother I have always respected. For the past seven years, she has loved and accepted me unconditionally, and has offered me compassionate words of wisdom. She knew I was at the end of my rope, and encouraged me to take *time-out* and focus on the two most important issues in my life—my relationship with God, and rebuilding my marriage. I was so thankful to have a true friend who took the time to help me put my life back together again. I knew she was right—that, by rebuilding my foundation of God and family, everything else would somehow come back into order.

Friends in the Lord, Sheri and Leslie

Mark and Leslie have been through our struggles right along side us and have been steadfast in their faith and encouragement. Friends like that are rare and should be held tightly!

Chapter 29

The Calm After The Storm

After the bankruptcy, we had no visible means of support and I was determined to stay home with Jacob. I realized that for years, I hadn't trusted God to provide and kept jumping in His way. I finally reasoned, "My husband is fully capable and willing. Let *him* do the work!"

While Steve was searching for a new career, he took jobs as a freelance graphic designer, a waiter in a local restaurant, a limo driver and resumed professional modeling. Here was a man who had been running a production company, mingling with Hollywood industry professionals, and writing and producing. Now he was willing to do whatever it took to save our family. I can't tell you how much I grew to admire and respect my husband for being a man of such character. In just a short time of being home together, our marriage began to improve greatly.

I still, however, had some unfinished business to take care of at the Mrs. United States Headquarters. I called the National Director, "I'm sorry to tell you this, but I'm not going to be able to produce this year's Mrs. Arizona Pageant." As I started to make up excuses I realized that I needed to just be truthful. "The truth is, Isabella, I have Chronic Fatigue Syndrome, I just lost a baby, and our company was forced into bankruptcy." I was shocked by her response.

"That's okay, Sheri, why don't you just represent Arizona in the National Mrs. United States Pageant, since you've been in so many pageants before." For the first time in years, a spark of excitement hit my life again. I had always dreamed about becoming a National Titleholder! I even wondered if this was part of God's new plan for my life. I told Isabella that I would call her the next day after discussing this opportunity with my husband.

I could hardly wait for Steve to get home from work that day. I got so excited about being in this pageant that for a moment I forgot all the odds against me—I was 20 pounds overweight, in poor health, totally broke, and had no pageant wardrobe. Steve was so excited to see his normally depressed wife all lit up inside, that he was dying to know what was on my mind.

"I need a miracle, Honey," I exclaimed.

"Well, let's pray," he said. "What exactly is it that we're praying for?"

"Honey, I know we've had a tough time this year, but I've been offered an opportunity to represent Arizona in the 1994 Mrs. United States Pageant," I replied. I think he was so relieved to see that I still had some life left in me that he would have agreed to pray for almost anything. He also knew it was a dream of mine that I had given to God ten years ago. It was reassuring to see Steve show such confidence in me even though I had a lot of obstacles in my path. With complete submission to God, we got down on our knees and gave it to Him. We knew if it was His will He would bring it to pass.

I immediately dove for the phone and started calling for sponsors. I was amazed at the first phone call I made—the company offered to sponsor me the full entry fee without even requesting a written proposal.

"This is not normal!" I reminded myself as I thanked God. My next call was to a health club. I desperately needed a fitness membership since I only had 8 weeks to lose 23 pounds. I then called a tanning salon, a manicurist, a chiropractor, a doctor for my chronic fatigue and all my needs were provided in less than 30 minutes of phone work! My dad even offered to rent the evening gown I needed for the competition. I knew the Lord had gone before me and I was thankful.

My biggest battle was overcoming my chronic fatigue so that I would have the energy to exercise and get in shape. A doctor introduced me to an incredible health and wellness system called Body Wise. Their products literally turned my health completely around! I lost 23 pounds in eight weeks, my skin cleared up, and I had more energy than I had ever experienced before!

Thanks to the help of my husband, some wonderful friends and a merciful God, I felt like I was out of a storm. Why didn't God keep me out of it all along? I was growing to realize that God's plan for my personal growth is to take me *through* the storms and not keep me out of them. Only then would I learn to trust Him.

Chapter 30

The Crown That Was Left at the Cross

The night before the pageant, as I was packing, I reflected on the previous eight weeks and knew in my heart I had done my very best to prepare. I got down on my knees and thanked God for this opportunity. I then prayed, "Lord, I give this completely to you. My life is in Your hands—storm or calm. May Your will be done."

The big day arrived—July 10, 1994. I was a basket-case as usual waiting to board the plane to Las Vegas. Yes, I'm afraid to fly! Even though I spent most of my adult life traveling, I always hated flying. I take that back—I hate crashing! It was funny to me that I was more afraid of a simple one-hour flight than I was of competing with 51 contestants for a national title.

On the plane, I sat next to a fascinating Christian woman from Arkansas named Myrtle Guise. She was on her way to celebrate her 80th birthday with her family in Las Vegas. Have you ever noticed that women seem to have the gift of being able to talk and listen simultaneously? With both of us sitting practically face-to-face and talking at the same time, Myrtle and I each shared our life stories in one hour. Early on, she informed me that she was writing a book about the many miracles God had done in her life. I was so relieved to hear this—now I knew the plane couldn't possibly crash, because she had to finish her book!

She asked me why I was competing, and I told her the story of how God had brought me to this point, and how I wanted to use this for His glory. I was so totally at ease with Myrtle— like she had known me forever! Slowly she took my hand, held it tightly and said very deliberately and plainly, "Sheri Rose, I'm going to give you the phone number of the place I'll be staying at in Las Vegas. I want you to call me on Saturday night, because you're going to win that crown! God is going to give you back the crown you left at the Cross ten years ago, and He's going to use your story to restore hope to hurting people across the nation!" Then, she gently kissed me on the forehead and said with a smile, "Remember Who's with you."

I was in awe of this woman! She had such peace and conviction—did she know something I didn't? In my lifetime, I've flown in countless planes to dozens of places, but I will never forget that one hour airplane ride to Las Vegas.

Because I still had five more pounds to lose, during the five days of the pageant, I ate nothing but tuna, vegetable juice, and the Body Wise supplements. Each morning, I would ask God to use me to encourage someone that day, and He always did. In fact, it got to the point where I started feeling like the pageant chaplain! It was worth it, though, because some of the women I talked to decided to recommit their lives to God.

Friday evening was the preliminary night to the main event on Saturday. The swimsuit competition was first on the program. I'd always hated this part of the pageant! Why do they make women parade around in swimsuits and be judged for it? It isn't as though the winner is ever again going to wear a swimsuit in connection with her reign. In any case, I started feeling quite insecure, and forgot the real reason why I was there and Who had brought me this far. My insecurities killed my performance that night. I was in fifteenth place, which wasn't even high enough to pull me into the ten semi-finalists for Saturday night's final competition.

After the preliminaries wrapped up later that evening, I returned to my room disappointed and exhausted. As I got ready for bed, I heard a knock at the door. It was one of the contestants I'd been sharing with during the week.

"I'm sorry to bother you, Sheri, but I really need to talk," she pleaded.

"Just a minute." I said, excusing myself long enough to fetch a robe and to pray a quick prayer, "Lord, if this is Your will that I stay up to talk to her, please don't let me have puffy eyes in the morning!"

I stayed up talking with her until about 1:00 a.m., then tried to get some much needed sleep. Unfortunately, my scheduled interview with the panel of judges was at 8:00 a.m. the next morning—only a few hours away!

The judges interview consisted of a one minute speech by the contestant, followed by five minutes of questioning from the panel. The interview was 50% of our total score, therefore, because of my poor showing in last night's preliminary, I knew I had to do extremely well in this segment of competition in order to become one of the ten semi-finalists.

Right before the interview the next morning, Steve met me in the lobby with flowers and some encouraging words. He knew I was disappointed and a little drained. He then took my copy of the speech I'd prepared and said, "Forget about this. Just go in there and do what you do best—speak from your heart. I'm going to pray with you right now, and everything's going to turn out great." Boy, was he right! As I spoke to the judges from my heart, they laughed and they cried. I knew I had an incredible interview! (I later found out that I won the overall interview competition by 36 points).

It was an incredibly long Saturday, but at last the show was ready to begin. All the contestants were finally lined up backstage waiting to be ushered on stage for the start of the telecast. I did a quick mental calculation of how much time we had before going on, and then motioned to one of the chaperones. "I need to pray." I told her.

"Are you out of your mind? There's no time for that!" she responded.

"I have to!" I insisted, and ran off to the nearest restroom. On my knees, I told God, "If You let me win this crown tonight, I'll only use it for You. Help me to do my best, and *Your* will be done, Lord, not mine."

I know that we're not supposed to bargain with God—like *Let's Make a Deal* or something—but, I just felt the need to verbalize my commitment to give *everything* to Him.

When we reached the countdown of the top ten finalists, none of the ladies dared breathe as we listened and hoped to hear our names called. One by one they announced the names of the chosen few, and my hopes began to dwindle as they called out eight of the ten finalists and I was not among them. But the ninth name called was mine. I started to cry as if I'd won. I was in shock!

At this point, all our scores were reset to zero, and the last three phases of the pageant began with on-stage interviews of the ten semi-finalists. I was first. The question I drew was, "What is it about your generation that you are most proud of?"

"Unlike the 'ME' generation of the '80s, my generation

is realizing how important it is to think about more than just themselves. We're going back to the basics, putting more emphasis on families and relationships. We're finally realizing that this life is short, and we need to make each moment count," I answered, acknowledged the judges, and managed a somewhat awkward grin as I heard my "fans" hooting and hollering from the audience. (My friends, family and some of my pageant girls filled up four rows, and definitely made their voices heard!)

Next, it was back into the swimsuits. I thought the other nine ladies were decidedly more beautiful than I, but I managed to get through it alright. Finally, it was time for the evening gown competition (My husband escorted me, and this time, I think *he* got the applause!). As this concluded, we were all whisked back onstage to wait for the names of the winners.

I could feel my hands trembling as I stood anxiously on stage with the other girls, waiting, smiling, under what felt like a thousand heat lamps. The master of ceremonies held up the envelope containing the names of the winners and announced, "We started our search for the new Mrs. United States with thousands of women from around the nation, and 51 of them won the right to represent their states here this week. From those 51, the number has been narrowed to ten semi-finalists, who have competed in tonight's competition..."

The thousand lights seemed to blend together now into a vicious beam focused right at me. My hands were now sweating and my heart was racing. "Just keep your balance and smile!" I said to myself. The announcer continued,

"We will now take that number from ten to five as we announce our four runners-up and our new Mrs. United States. I will start with the name of the fourth runner-up."

As the drum-roll began, my stomach started churning into a giant knot, my arms went numb, and I was certain that my hyper-ventilating would pop the sequins off my evening gown! Still, I waited. I smiled. Each time the announcer called the name of one of the four runners-up, I listened for "Arizona", but, it wasn't to be.

After he announced the name of the first runner-up, I was left standing with five other contestants. Two of them were women I thought had the best chances of winning, so as the announcer cleared his throat to proclaim the winner, I prepared myself to hear one of their names. As the six of us looked on, not daring to move or breathe, the announcer said, "Our new Mrs. United States of America is...Mrs. Arizona! Sheri Rose Shepherd!"

In that instant, when I heard my name, I felt like a spring loaded catapult launched me off the stage and into a screaming sea of emotion. I screamed, I cried, I shook like a giant, beaded baby rattle in heels! I lost all of the control and composure I had been trying to display during the competition. I couldn't believe I won!

After the pageant, all the contestants seemed to flood me with love and support. Then, after what seemed like countless photos, my husband whisked me away to celebrate my new victory at the MGM Grand with my son, Jacob, my dad and his new wife, Irina, my brother, Michael, many of my sponsors, quite a few old friends, and one other very special guest—my mom. It meant so much to me to have her there, after all we'd been through.

It was two o'clock in the morning by the time I got back to my room, but despite the late hour, I just had to make one phone call.

"Myrtle, I'm so sorry to wake you, but it's Sheri from the airplane. You were right. I won the crown! I'm the new Mrs. United States!"

"I'm so excited for you, Sheri!" she beamed. "When you were telling me your story on the plane, I knew God had brought you through a great battle to give you an even greater victory," she told me. "I knew God let me live 80 years for a reason. I'm going to spend the *rest of my life* covering you in prayer. I love you, Sheri, and I'm proud of you."

I hung up the phone and sleepily wiped more tears from my eyes. I set my crown and banner on the table by the window, turned out the lights and tried to sleep. As the miraculous events of the evening—and of my life—ran through my mind, I looked up and noticed a beam of light shining through a slit in the curtains, illuminating my new crown and banner. I stared at the symbols of my victory and started to cry. I thought, "I've never shed so many tears in my life—I take that back—I've never shed so many *happy* tears in my life!"

I knew then that all those things God had pulled me through during my life were to prepare me for this time. As I drifted off to sleep, I recalled Myrtle's words from the plane trip, "This is the beginning of a *new* plan God has for your life. Remember Who's with you."

> Remember not the former things,
>   nor consider the things of old.
> Behold, I will do a new thing;
>   now it springs forth, do you not perceive it?
> I will make a way in the wilderness,
>   and rivers in the desert.
>
> Isaiah 43:18

My new friend, Myrtle, shared with me a life-time of hope on one short plane flight.

I will relive this moment in my mind forever, but I will always remember Who gave it to me.

I am very grateful to Body Wise, International for their wonderful nutritional products, and their unshakable faith in me.

I appreciate the national and local media for sharing my story of hope with people across the country.

*An interview
for Inside
Edition at
our home in
Phoenix.*

*The 700 Club,
live in Virginia
Beach.*

*My son,
Jacob, was
my official
"flag waver"
on Fox TV in
Sacramento.*

*I love working
with children!
They possess so
much wonder.
They're also my
best "fans"*

*My pageant daughters
did a lot of volunteer
work in the community.*

*The Salvation Army
Youth Camp with 350
young people.*

*Signing
autographs
at Planet
Hollywood.*

Guest Speaker at the "Women Who Make A Difference" Conference.

Backstage with Steven Curtis Chapman and my sister-in-law, Susan.

With my favorite actress, "Alice" (Ann B. Davis) from everyone's dream family, The Brady Bunch.

My mom, Carole, joined us while I spoke seven different times over Mother's Day weekend.

Mike MacIntosh and his lovely wife at the Youth Development Int. Conference for the Youth Crisis Hotline.

Closing Thoughts

I once read a survey which indicated that 96% of the population did indeed believe in God. If you happen to be one of the remaining 4%, I appreciate that you hung in there with me until the end, even though the later chapters became increasingly God-centered. Obviously, that was because my *life* became increasingly God-centered. I discovered that the more I moved the central focus of my life off of myself and onto Him, the better my life became.

For those among the 96%, there are no doubt some whose views on God are different from my own. Please know that, in relaying my own experiences, I certainly have no wish to offend anyone, and I hope you're able to take it all in the spirit in which it's intended.

Whatever you believe or don't believe about God, I hope you'll consider for a moment that, if God is indeed real, He deserves to be the center of all of our lives, even if giving Him His rightful place meant no gain whatsoever for us. But the fact is—every single person I've ever known who truly made Jesus "Number One" in their life, has been transformed for the better by His power. Not everyone's initial experiences with God will be quite as dramatic as mine, but you can be certain that His plan for your life is the right one.

There's no way to convince you of all of this

intellectually, however. So let me challenge you to do one simple thing. Before you close this book for the final time, ask God to show you if He is truly real, and if what I've been telling you about Him is true. What do you have to lose? If He's there (and I know He is), He'll find a way to show you that He's there for you, and that He loves you so much that He even sent His Son to die for you to give you access to Him forever. Perhaps the mere fact that you've read my book is one of the evidences that God has been trying to get your attention.

Please know that I have already been praying for you, since I pray each morning for Him to bless everyone who reads this book. If you have any questions about anything you've read here or elsewhere in the book, don't hesitate to write to me, and I'll do my best to get an answer to you.

Sheri Rose Shepherd

Write to:
Shepherd Marketing
15111 N. Hayden Suite 160
Scottsdale, Arizona 85260

Acknowledgements

Almost always when someone conquers a Great Victory in their life, there are many people that share in that victory. In my case, the list is endless of the incredible people who invested their time in my life and unselfishly gave of themselves.

I want to personally acknowledge my love and appreciation for the following people:

Steven Gene Shepherd   *Karen & Doug Ray*
Jacob Andrew Shepherd   *Myrtle Guise*
Carole Goodman   *Dr. David Gregg*
Phil Goodman   *Dr. William Tikey*
Barbara & Chandler Peterson   *Thomas T. Tierney*
Mark & Leslie Bundy   *Ray Grimm*
Marc Rebboah   *Scott Hart*
Tommy & Marja Barnett   *Dr. Kevin Harris*
Scott & Anna Ruiz   *Lana Krug*
Joyce Wells   *Emily & Charlie*
Karen Kennedy   *Kay Hansen*
Connie & Dick Huggins   *Greg Ochinero*
Susie Goodman   *Steve Brown*
Dr. Eckel   *...and most importantly,*
Jan & Everitt Shepherd   *God, for giving me a*
Susan & Derrick Tuten   *new life.*

Special Thanks to Tom DiBiase. Tom is a freelance writer living in Scottsdale, Arizona. If you want to discuss writing projects with Tom, you can write to him at P.O. Box 6158, Scottsdale, AZ 85261

As a Christian Evangelist, I constantly meet people in desperate need of direction. People who are suffering from chronic depression, eating disorders, substance abuse, teen pregnancy, obesity, and health problems. I have listed a few resources that I highly recommend.. This is not to take the place of prayer and the study of God's Word, and although I am not a doctor or a professional counselor, I do encourage you to set your goals and make a plan on how you are going to conquer them.

Please Call...If You Need Help

Suicide, Runaways, Abuse
Youth Crisis Hotline
(800) HIT-HOME

•

Eating Disorders
New Life Treatment Center
(800) NEW-LIFE

•

Drug and Alcohol Abuse
Teen Challenge
(520) 292-2273

•

Teen Pregnancy
Crisis Pregnancy Center
(602) 829-0398

•

Health Enhancement or Weight Loss
Body Wise International
Independent Consultant
(602) 404-1507

Additional copies of
"Who Would Have Thought..."
and
Steve and Sheri Shepherd's devotional book
"Challenging You to Excellence"
are available from:

Shepherd Publications
15111 North Hayden Road
Suite 160-242
Scottsdale, AZ 85260

"Who Would Have Thought..." $12.95 (US) $16.95 (CAN)

"Challenging You to Excellence" $10.95 (US) $13.95 (CAN)

Please add $2.00 ea. for shipping and handling

Bulk orders, autographed copies, or any additional
information may be obtained by calling:

(602) 407-8789